CAMPING
IN COMFORT

CAMPING IN COMFORT

a guide
to modern
outdoor vacations

NORMAN
and SIL
STRUNG

J. B. LIPPINCOTT COMPANY
Philadelphia & New York

Line drawings are by Virginia Munn.

This one's for Tom Sicard, with whom we've shared the pleasure of countless campfires and who taught us a great, great deal.

Preface

Although a relatively small percentage of our population consider themselves outdoorsmen, everyone participates in some kind of outdoor activity no matter how citified he may think he is. The family Sunday drive into the country is an outdoor activity; it's a drive to find a small part of the peace, privacy, and satisfaction that a camping family finds on a week end in a shady glen. The elderly couple with the green thumb who grow plants and flowers in window boxes are outdoorsmen at heart too. They enjoy on a smaller scale the satisfaction a camper has with each new morning. The child who toys with mud pies, the young mother who spends an afternoon with her child on a park bench, and the businessman who walks four blocks instead of taking the subway are all potential campers too. Everyone should enjoy camping, yet many are reluctant to try it. They view a stay in the outdoors as it was decades ago: a contest between man and the wilderness fit only for the young, the dedicated, and the expert. And they're very wrong.

The past ten years have totally changed the face of camping just as surely as the past twenty years have changed the pace of living. Convenience and comfort have spread from the kitchen to the cookstove, from the bedroom to the sleeping bag, and from the living room to the camping trailer. The modern camper can spend a night in an improved campsite complete with showers, electricity, and laundry service. If he wants to go it alone, he can get off the beaten track and park his truck camper in the deepest woods, and he'll still have all the comforts of home without lifting a finger because, like a turtle, he's brought his home with him. In short, a combination of necessity, invention, and demand has created a whole new kind of camping suited to all tastes and all ages. It includes dehydrated foods and compact mobile homes, catalytic heaters and pop-up tents, paper sleeping bags and sleek snowmobiles. It's modern, it's what's happening.

Modern camping—what it is and how to achieve total comfort in your outdoor vacation—is what this book is all about. If you're looking for old Indian remedies or want to know how to build a shelter out of snow, better put this back on the rack; you won't find that kind of information here.

But if you're the kind of person who wants to enjoy the outdoors without fighting it, if you'd rather spend your time tempting a trout or just watching the progress of a season instead of hacking out a camp with an axe and a knife, then read on. This book is written for you.

Acknowledgments

Credit is due our many friends who are supporting members of the Outdoor Writers Association of America. They were of immeasurable help through the information they provided and the advice they gave. Special thanks go to John Ebeling of Winnebago, C. H. Manchester of Airstream, the BernzOmatic Corporation, Paulin Infra-Red Products Company, G. A. Cunningham of Colorado Outdoor Sports Corporation, Charlie McIllwaine of the Coleman Company, and Charlie Grant of Vesely.

Some very special thanks go to 200-odd nameless campers. Tolerant souls all, they allowed us to poke around, pry into, and thoroughly inspect their assorted outdoor homes. They taught us tricks it would have taken a lifetime to learn on our own, and provided us with a unique source of accurate, practical information on modern camping gear and techniques.

Contents

Photographs follow page 128

CAMPING
IN COMFORT

1 Planning the Trip

Wade Lake is to us the most beautiful place in the world. It's a glacial lake: a delicate diamond that's locked in a setting of steep, fir-studded banks and worn on the finger of a tributary of Montana's Madison River. It lies just under the rim of the Continental Divide and is brooded over by a magnificent mountain that keeps its cap of snow for ten months out of the year.

Sil and I camp there every spring, in a little lakeside swale where the grass is as thick as a carpet. We get there by way of outboard . . . a trip across the lake from the launching site and public campground. It's a little extra work, but we think it's worth the effort.

The setting is solitude . . . plain and simple. Only jumping trout and an occasional deer or bear are to be seen there. That's why we love it so. But our camp is hardly plain and simple. When we invite friends to come along, they're never less than astounded at how comfortable our brand of "roughing it" really is. They usually show up with visions of canvas lean-tos, of sleeping on the ground and hunching around a fire. They leave with memories of

1

CAMPING IN COMFORT

quilted air mattresses, soft as any feather bed, deck chairs, a sheltered eating area, gourmet meals, and, yes, even martinis at five. Invariably, sometime during their stay, someone will pipe up with, "How do you do it? How can a guy pack so much comfort and convenience into the outdoors?"

To that question, our usual answer is, "Friend, it would take a book to explain it all, but for a start. . . ."

Camping can amount to an ordeal or a vacation, depending on how you do it. The great bulk of Americans want all the comfort they can cram into their camping. For all of us, successful, enjoyable living in the outdoors depends on a lot of things—planning, outdoor savvy, knowing the equipment to bring and how to use it, to name just a few. All of them play a part at one time or another. And when you mix these ingredients with liberal doses of grass, trees, fresh air, clean water, and the heat of the sun, the result is sweet indeed.

WHAT KIND OF CAMPING FOR YOU?

Learning to live comfortably under canvas or on wheels is a little like baking a cake. When you start from scratch as a cook, you've got to find the flour. When you're planning on doing some outdoor living, your basic ingredient should be finding the brand of camping that suits you best.

Campers are newlyweds on their honeymoon, sleeping in the back of a station wagon and cooking their meals over a portable stove so they can save money. Campers are a retired couple, fulfilling a long dream by touring the nation in the living-room luxury of a motor home. Or a family on a week-end jaunt, lugging a tent trailer and a carful of kids down to the sea. Or a group of mountaineers with packs on their backs and their eyes focused on a sky-scraping mountain peak. Or surfcasters with a plastic lean-to on the beach . . . deer hunters living in a tent city . . . a family on a houseboat moving up the Mississippi. What kind of camper are you? And where do you begin? You decide first what you expect of camping.

Few people are satisfied with pitching their tents or parking their trailers, then sitting around all day "camping." Camping is a pastime that's a welcome and necessary adjunct to other activities. And because it lends itself so well to so many things, the approaches to camping, the equipment available, and the jobs that equipment will accomplish are as diversified as the great outdoors.

Do your interests run toward sight-seeing? Have you longed to tour our national parks? Would you like to test and savor the depth and breadth of a big country that stretches its arms all the way from the Maine coast, across the plains of Kansas, to the Sierra Madres of California? If those are your leanings, then the mobile comfort of trailers, truck campers, and motor homes might be for you.

Convenience is another consideration. Just how much of it do you like? If you're the kind of guy who loves his living room and doesn't enjoy the kind of work involved in pitching a tent and putting together a camp, whether you're a sight-seer or not, you'll be wise to investigate self-contained auto campers.

How about those who will be traveling with you? If you have several young children, the civilized amenities of hot and cold running water, toilets, kitchen-performance stoves and refrigerators make life a lot easier. Again, this points to units on wheels.

On the other hand, if your budget is limited, if you like to get away from it all, and you enjoy the crackle of a campfire as a companion on fishing and hunting trips, then the low price, compactness, and portability of tents would better suit your tastes.

Perhaps your children are teen-agers with ambitions to paddle a canoe, climb a mountain, or hike along the seashore. That's tent territory too.

Although all these variations of camping will be discussed at length a little later in this book, here's a brief list of the kinds of outdoor living accommodations a modern camper can expect. Compare what they'll do with what you want them to, and you'll at least be in your general camping neighborhood.

MOTOR HOMES are houses built over a set of wheels. They range in size from small, converted utility vans up to plush palaces built on a bus frame. The small units are the most mobile of the auto campers. They also pack the fewest conveniences. The big ones are the ultimate in comfort, but they can't navigate beyond paved roads. Prices range from $3,500 for the small stuff all the way up to a whopping $18,000 for a home with "the works."

TRAVEL TRAILERS involve the same limitations, conveniences, and cost range (when you figure the price of the towing vehicle) as motor homes. They have the advantage of greater flexibility in that the living quarters can be separated from the transportation.

TRUCK CAMPERS make you something of a turtle. You carry your home in the bed of, or bolted to, a truck chassis. They can be bought with all the equipment travel trailers and motor homes have, but they're a bit more cramped than either. Prices on a suitable truck start at around $3,000. Costs of campers range from $400 for a bare-walled "shell" to luxury units at $3,500.

CAMPER TRAILERS, also called tent trailers, amount to collapsible travel trailers. By the turn of a crank, the roof goes up and walls of plastic and canvas blossom out. They're quite roomy for their size, and at costs that run from $350 to $2,000, budget-priced as well.

BOATS are more practical than most people realize, especially if water sports are your forte. Small boats can be used in conjunction with tents. Most of the large, live-on boats incorporate all the comforts of a medium-sized auto camper and can be used as a home both on the trailer and in the water. Prices for suitable live-on craft, including motors and trailers, start at around $4,000.

FAMILY-SIZED TENTS offer a lot of room and portability for a low price, but require the most work, not only in setting up, but in packing and unpacking accessories. Depending on size, tents cost between $70 and $300 and, in addition, you have to buy the gear that goes with tent camping. Estimate for a family of four: around $600 for a topnotch outfit.

LIGHTWEIGHT MOUNTAIN TENTS are small and light and offer a minimum of living comfort. Packed on your back, they'll go anywhere with you, along with the rest of the camping gear necessary for foot travel. But small doesn't mean cheap. Good mountain gear is more expensive than most people imagine: $70 for a two-man tent, $80 for a sleeping bag, $50 for a pack frame and sack, and so on.

TRIAL RUNS

"If the shoe fits, wear it," goes an old saying, but how do you tell if the thing fits without trying it on first?

If you're just getting into the camping game, you'll be making a minimum investment of $600, and plunking down a lot more if living on wheels is more to your liking. While it's certainly a good idea to research the possibilities and potentials of individual camping units by reading a printed page, talking to other campers, and paying a few visits to sports stores, you're not going to know the entire story until you actually live in your decision for a few days.

Once you have some ideas about the kind of camping that suits you best, try to arrange a trip with a friend who has a similar setup. If none of your friends are campers, rental agencies have the equipment to give you a telling taste of what you're considering biting off.

There are many companies that rent camping gear of all varieties; A-Z Rental is a nationwide chain that keeps a good supply of tenting gear on hand. KOA campgrounds often include trailer rentals with their campground operations. Several of the "you-drive-it" trailer and trucking firms offer both camper pickups and trailers for rent, and so do the "rent-a-car" agencies.

When it comes to costs, figure $12 to $24 rental a day

for a travel trailer. A pickup truck camper rents for $20 to $40 a day plus mileage. The prices are commensurate with the conveniences included in the package, and the roominess of the unit.

Tenting costs, inclusive of all the gear that goes with it, run between $60 and $80 a week for a family of four. In all rentals, there's usually a minimum charge amounting to three or four days' use.

One particularly good rental plan, offered by many dealers, is rental with an option to buy. You choose the unit you'd like to use, live with it for a while, and if you're satisfied with its performance, the rent you pay at trip's return will be applied to the purchase price of the entire package. This often is enough for a down payment.

PLANNING THE TRIP

Any successful camping trip begins long before you lock your door and climb behind the wheel. There are a hundred details, some large, some small, that will require your attention before you can be assured of a safe, enjoyable trip. Those details, and the time it takes to plan, increase proportionately with the length of your proposed outing.

If a short week-end trip to a nearby campground lies somewhere in the future, collecting and categorizing gear the week end before isn't too soon.

If you're planning on an entire vacation's worth of camping, laying the groundwork three months in advance is by no means too early. This is partly because a long trip into unfamiliar country requires some writing exercises (more about that later), but more important, when you're not in

7

a hurry and under the pressure of a deadline, matters of organization and details have a way of popping into your head with surprising ease.

And as soon as you start thinking about your camp out, here's a good way to keep track of what you come up with:

Post a sheet of paper in some prominent place in your home. As soon as you think of some gear to bring or receive some important bit of information or get an idea, write it down. Later you can translate it into a grocery list, gear-to-bring list, travel log, or whatever, but keep that piece of paper in plain sight. When it's there and easy to get at, all your companions will be quick to use it. When it's tucked in some drawer, or is part of a notebook, the temptation is to say, "I'm too busy to write it down now . . . I'll remember it for later."

But you seldom do.

Attention to detail will make the difference between comfortable convenience and uncomfortable make-do on your future trip. But for now, let's put specific details aside for a few pages and turn to some broader considerations that will influence and define your outing in its early stages of planning.

The first factor isn't what you can do . . . it's what you can't.

KNOW YOUR LIMITATIONS. All of us are subject to some limitations. I can't run the four-minute mile, Sil can't cook creamed corn without burning it, and nobody can spend more than he earns . . . at least not for very long.

One of the popular myths about camping is that it doesn't cost a cent. It is economical—but it's not for free.

When you're on the road, figure roughly $3 per person per day for food, $2 to $4 worth of gas and oil for every hundred miles of travel. Plan on a minimum of a dollar a night in public campgrounds, $3 a night in commercial operations.

And don't forget tolls, entrance fees to national parks, and incidentals like fishing licenses, souvenirs, ice-cream cones here and there, and the possibility of road emergencies.

Generally, a family of four will spend $25 to $30 a day if they're on the road, $15 to $20 a day if they set up camp and stay in one spot.

So get out your bankbook and, long before you settle on a faraway place with an attractive name, see if you can afford the outlay to get you there and back. And whatever the estimated cost of the trip comes to, add another hundred dollars to it, just to be on the safe side.

The quality, kind, and thoroughness of your equipment are other kinds of limitations. If you're pulling a large trailer, you're not going to be able to explore the back country around Wyoming's Jackson Hole or drive on the rutted sand roads of the Cape May seashore. You simply can't get close enough with your "camp." You'd be much wiser to plan a trip that investigates the roadside wonders of Yellowstone National Park or the developed accesses that lie on the shores of great man-made lakes.

On the other hand, the mobility and pitch-it-anywhere nature of a tent are great for hard-to-get-to places, but if you're a touring "gypsy" camper, interested in seeing a lot of country in a relatively short time, living under canvas will drive you up a tent wall. You'll most likely be pitching and breaking a new camp every day. The extensive work required to set up a comfortable tent camp wears thin in a hurry when you do it too often.

This brings us to another kind of limitation, largely psychological.

How much camping can you and your family take in one big bite before outdoor living becomes a chore instead of a pleasure? How many miles can you plan to cover in a day without everyone getting too restless?

It's a difficult question to answer because every human is a little different from his neighbor. But here are a few figures that have evolved through our personal experience:

• Driving alone, 300 miles a day is about my comfort limit. With Sil to spell me, I'll shoot for 400 to 450 miles.

• Wilderness camping, when we're far removed from showers, central heating, ice cream, and television, is great for a week provided the weather's pleasant. In the cool spring and fall or in showery conditions, more than four days is too much.

• Tent camping with a road nearby—a road that provides access to a hot shower and fresh groceries—five days to a week and a half, depending on the weather.

• Campers or travel trailers with moderate appointments (no showers or toilet) account for pleasant living for up to a week and a half without a break.

• Motor homes and large trailers with complete self-containment take quite a while before you tire of them. Although we've never used them for that long a period, we estimate a month or two on the road wouldn't be too much.

Now I know there's some explanation due here. First, when I talk about our psychological limitations, I don't mean to imply that, after four days of solid rain in the wilderness, or 350 miles behind the wheel without a break, or two weeks in a small camper, you will lose your marbles.

What I do mean is that, after that ill-defined period I call "comfortable," the mountains begin to gradually lose their glamour, the enthusiasm to make another fifty miles starts to ebb, and you just don't look quite so favorably toward reaching the next campsite, even though it's smack-dab in the middle of the best steelhead fishing hole in the West.

Instead, your thoughts gently turn toward a hot shower, crisp bed linens, a full-course meal with salad and apple pie, and the admitted inanities of network TV. You say things like, "Man, won't it feel great to relax for a change . . ." even though that's what you've been doing all along.

This doesn't mean that if you want to tent camp for a month, you're going to hate the last two weeks. It does mean that although we hairy-chested outdoorsmen hate to admit it, a shower, an inner-spring mattress, and a permanent roof over our heads feel pretty good once in a while.

So to fully enjoy your camping trip, plan on breaking up the day-after-day outdoor life with at least a few "treats" via a motel, hotel, or luxury commercial campground. And don't forget that those treats should find a place on your tally sheet when you're figuring up your financial limitations.

THE SHAKEDOWN CRUISE. Those observations about "comfortable limits" are admittedly a personal rule of thumb, so to explore your own limits and tastes, and fifty other factors pertinent to your brand of camping, the "shakedown

11

cruise"—getting your camping feet wet before you dive in —is a wise move in terms of long-trip planning.

Even if you've got some experience under your belt, taking one or two experimental outings previous to a major trip is a wise move. It's a chance to try out any new or unfamiliar equipment you might have bought in the past year, a good way to check the condition and performance of old equipment, a refresher course on camping techniques, and a just plain fun way to spend a few spare days.

Start your shakedown camping out in small stages. Take an overnighter before you tackle a full week end, and try that two-day week end before you go camping on a long holiday. Learn about your equipment, and how to use camping tricks and techniques in easy-to-digest doses. Don't "cram" the night before leaving . . . you're sure to fail the test.

If you've never camped before, even your shakedown cruise should be planned with all the odds in your favor. Make it a short trip. If you can sneak the time off, plan it for the middle of the week when campgrounds and campsites won't be crowded, and when roads won't be overloaded.

Weather is important too. At least on that first trip, make every effort to try out your camping legs during the sunny, warm weather. Of course, no one has yet come up with a hundred-per-cent infallible weather prediction, but if the days you've selected for your trial run come attached to a forecast for wet weather, cancel the trip and try for another time.

The place you pick for a campsite is important too. Even

12

though one of the greatest joys of camping is when you can "get away from it all," as a neophyte you'd be much wiser to pick a spot that boasts of conveniences such as tables, graded tent sites, running water, toilet facilities, and stores.

As a matter of fact, the very best campsite for that first outing is in your own backyard.

No, we're not joking. What better way to familiarize yourself with new equipment? Unfamiliar cooking techniques? The art of sleeping comfortably in a sleeping bag? Then, if something does go wrong—say your tent pegs pull out during a thunderstorm and the whole thing comes crashing down at 3 A.M.—all you've got to do is walk to your house and you're back in your own bed.

Backyard camping might not seem too exciting, but it's eminently practical for the beginner for one very important reason. It's awfully easy to get turned off to outdoor living if too many things go wrong on the first trip out. I've seen it happen more than once, and because of things that might seem inconsequential: a forgotten salt shaker or pillow for your head, a tent pitched in the wrong place, or a trailer parked at the wrong angle.

Even with the best equipment and a modern campground, a beginner, unfamiliar with how to cope with minor campsite inconveniences, soon assumes they're major and unavoidable camping pains in the neck. From there, it's a mistaken but common step to decide that camping is too uncomfortable for him.

WHAT TO DO—WHERE TO GO. When you're a camper, the world is truly your oyster. The activities you can devise and

13

participate in are limited only by your imagination. Sea-coasts, rivers, lakes, mountains, swamps, plains—you can put yourself into any one of those worlds and in each have multiple choices of recreational activities. Indeed, there are so many camping-associated possibilities for fun that any family can be hard pressed to decide which they prefer. If you have trouble narrowing down just where you want to go, here's an interesting exercise that everybody will enjoy.

Thumb through the pages of a lot of camping, travel, and outdoor magazines. (A particularly good place to look is Woodall's *Travel-Camping the Four Seasons*, a state-by-state listing of activities campers can enjoy during every season of the year. Rand McNally publishes a similar guide and both are available in any bookstore.) Each time you come across a place or activity that looks interesting, write it down on a piece of paper. Make sure to include ideas from everybody in your camping clan during the search. Chances are you'll come up with at least a dozen ideas, not just from the magazines—there will probably be a few original notions that will pop into participants' heads. Once you get a varied selection of people, places, activities, and ideas, it's time to narrow things down.

Your selection, in part, might read something like this:

Tennessee, TVA Lakes: fishing for bass

Yellowstone National Park: sight-seeing

New York, Fire Island National Seashore: swimming, surfing, fishing

Minnesota, Ely: canoeing, fishing, wilderness camping

South Dakota, Black Hills, Mount Rushmore, Badlands: sight-seeing

14

Florida, Keys and Everglades: sight-seeing, water sports
Kansas, Salinas: visit Aunt Emma and Uncle John
West Virginia, Smoky Mountains: sight-seeing, hiking

As a for instance, let's say you live in Buffalo, New York. Your vacation budget is a little tight this year, thanks to the purchase of a new car and all that camping equipment, so you've got a financial limitation that warns against a long journey. Scratch Yellowstone, Minnesota, and the Black Hills. They involve a long trip. Then you remember that no one in the family enjoys hot muggy weather. So scratch Florida until you can take a camping trip in cooler weather. Then your wife remembers that Aunt Emma and Uncle John are planning a cross-country camping trip to stay with *you* for a week. Scratch Salinas.

That leaves three choices: Tennessee, West Virginia, and Long Island. If you can all reach agreement on one place to go, fine. If not, you can draw straws, or use whatever other method works best in your family to make final decisions.

PLANNING THE ITINERARY

You know when, where, and for how long you'll be camping, but you know very little else. Maybe your reading has told you about campgrounds at your destination, but what kind of facilities can you count on along the way? What's the best route . . . the fastest, the most scenic? What kind of weather can you expect?

These are all questions that need answers, and the quickest, most reliable way to find them is by letter or telephone.

Pick your travel route first, and don't do it yourself.

15

CAMPING IN COMFORT

Though it's easy for anyone to find the shortest distance between two points on a road map, what do you know about possible road construction? Or routes that look fast, but indeed are dotted with bottlenecks?

For that kind of information, turn to any of the auto clubs. If you're a member of something like the AAA (Automobile Association of America), the service is free. If you're a non-member, plotting your best route will involve a small charge.

Many major oil companies are more than willing to provide this service, too, and usually for free. If you hold one of their credit cards, mention this and they'll pinpoint their stations along the way, so you can plan in advance for gas stops. You might also mention the kind of pace you're planning to set. Do you want to get to your destination in a hurry and spend most of your time there, or are you more interested in a leisurely drive that takes in plenty of scenery and pleasant, though slow, back-country roads?

Once you know your route and your total mileage, it's time for more specifics. Assuming you've introduced yourself to camping in gradual steps, you have a pretty good idea of how many miles you can and care to cover in a day. Whatever that mileage might be—200, 300, 400 miles a day—plot out that distance on a map and locate the nearest town. Establish an itinerary so you have some idea of what area will provide your camp every night. Then it's time to write a few letters.

Chambers of commerce in those towns where you plan to stop will be delighted to list any and all available campsites in their area. If you have some specific ideas in mind

—say a shower, or laundry day—mention that too, and they'll include information on where you can find these services. Perhaps you'd like to take a few days off at that point and just relax. They'll also tell you scenic points of interest, where to find hiking trails, and what to expect in the way of fishing. All you have to do is ask.

Although chambers of commerce have proven to be the most reliable source of up-to-date information for us, they're by no means the only source.

The U. S. Forest Service, Washington, D.C., maintains the best of the public campgrounds. Write them, tell them where you're planning to go, and they'll send you a listing of their nearby campgrounds.

States maintain public campgrounds too, and most of them have a published listing of all the sites inside their borders. Although the names of their recreation agencies differ (some are called Department of Fish and Game, some Department of Conservation, some Department of Recreation), addressing your letter to the state capitol using any one of these names will eventually get your request into the right hands.

There are also several magazines published that have a state-by-state listing of any and all campgrounds in a given area. They list both public and private campgrounds, and rate the commercial operations for quality and service. Rand McNally's effort in this area is called *Guidebook to Campgrounds*. Woodall publishes *Trailering Parks and Campgrounds*.

And if you still want to write some more, there's a list of other agencies in the last chapter of this book.

17

CAMPING IN COMFORT

When you're actually on the road, here are a few more things to remember that will help you find a spot for the night and have a more pleasant trip.

• Unless you're stopping at a commercial campground where you've made reservations, try to drive early and camp early. Popular campgrounds anywhere these days are usually filled up by 3 or 4 P.M., so the earlier you arrive, the better choice of campsites you'll have.

• Try to schedule your "rest breaks" for the week end and arrive early. On Saturday and Sunday, you'll find the most crowding on the roads, and the least number of available campsites for the family that doesn't stay put.

• Campgrounds near big water—lakes, rivers, and well-known trout streams—are always filled up before sites located in just plain woods.

MEDICAL CHECKUPS

Whether or not you're in the habit of having annual medical examinations, it's a good idea for every member of your family to have a checkup before setting out on your camping trip.

There's just an off-chance your doctor might come up with another kind of limitation to be included when you're laying your camping plans. Of course, it's most likely that he won't, but then you'll enjoy the extra plus of peace of mind.

Be sure to tell your doctor about the kind, length, and location of the trip you're planning. He can then check you out for things such as sun sensitivity, insect-bite reac-

18

tions, and, if you'll be in the mountains, how your heart will respond to high altitudes. Be sure to ask his advice on any shots you or your family might need for a worry-free vacation.

It's generally agreed that a tetanus booster is excellent and almost mandatory family protection. It's particularly important for campers to be protected from this disease, also called "lockjaw," for outdoor living in warm weather, barefoot and in shorts, is a combination that carries its share of scrapes, cuts, and punctures, especially around a campsite, and tetanus is an obvious risk under such conditions.

On certain occasions, diphtheria and typhoid boosters are also a wise move, particularly if you're considering a vacation jaunt into Canada or Mexico. If you'll be going into any other foreign country, you'll need a whole series of preventive shots.

Be sure to make this a part of your *initial* planning. All these shots can result in a reaction and fever for a few days. It's much better to endure those minor pains at home than on the first leg of a long vacation.

EXTRA PLANNING FOR CHILDREN AND PETS

If you are making the trip with young children, you hardly need to be reminded that games they can play in the car should be an important part of your luggage. You've probably had experience in traveling with them already and know what kinds of activities work best for them. If you're looking for new ideas, it's a good bet that the local toy

19

store, stationer, bookshop, or variety store will have a number of items specifically designed for children immobilized on auto trips.

Dogs and other pets may be no problem in the car or camper, but they require particular consideration in your planning. The states of Delaware, Maryland, Ohio, and Pennsylvania don't allow pets in state parks or state campgrounds, so if you're bringing your dog along on your trip, better plan on using commercial campgrounds when visiting within their boundaries. Most other states allow pets, but insist that dogs be kept leashed (a six-foot maximum) while on public property.

It's also a good idea to get a medical certificate of health and a rabies shot for your dog if you'll be crossing state lines. Both operations take a total of about 5 minutes, and cost in the neighborhood of $10. Some states require such certificates and inoculations.

And don't forget to keep a ready supply of water on hand for any animal who will be confined to a vehicle for long periods of time. There are several brands of splash-proof doggy dishes that won't leak a drop on the floor of your camper or car.

THE LOW-DOWN ON CAMPGROUNDS

Knowing what to expect of the campground you're going to be visiting next goes a long way toward providing a more enjoyable trip. Can you count on a shower when you get there? How about a store where you can pick up some extra groceries? Maybe you're tired of campgrounds where your neighbor pitches his tent an arm's length from your front door, and yearn for some scenic solitude?

Campgrounds fall into four basic categories. Each classification is at least an indication of the facilities and degree of "civilization" you can expect of them. The categories are: commercial campgrounds, improved public campgrounds, unimproved public campgrounds, and private campgrounds.

COMMERCIAL CAMPGROUNDS are privately owned businesses. They charge a per-night or per-week user fee, based on the number of people in your camping party. The charge is commensurate with the facilities and services provided by the campground.

The minimum-facility commercial operations usually include fixtures like fireplaces, picnic tables, graded tent sites, a ready wood supply, indoor toilets, pressurized water, and regular garbage collection. They cost in the neighborhood of $1.50 to $3.00 per night.

Moving up the scale of luxury, the more plush spots offer paved parking stalls, barbecue grills, sanitary and electric hookups for pickup campers and trailers, plus a central building that houses coin-operated laundry machines, ice machines, lavatories, and showers. They often include a general store where you can purchase foodstuffs and garden variety camping and cooking gear. These places can run anywhere from $3 to $7 a night for a family of four.

The real palaces include playgrounds, swimming pools, snack bars, and restaurants, and boast of recreation facilities like stocked fishing ponds and horseback riding and even evening entertainment. This kind of luxury costs. Figure $5 to $10 a night.

While there's plenty to be said for such fingertip convenience, it often incorporates a few drawbacks too. Many campers object to a commercial campground's usually crowded conditions. Then, too, they're often constructed in a less than natural outdoor setting. Because they're a business venture, they're far more likely to be next to a main highway than in some shady, out-of-the-way glen.

When we're on the road, rather than camping exclusively at commercial establishments, we like to use them once every three or four nights. It's an opportunity to take a shower, shop in nearby towns, and enjoy their luxuries as a kind of rest break from workaday camp chores. They're also handy when you have to drive late into the night since you can usually call ahead and make a reservation.

IMPROVED PUBLIC CAMPGROUNDS are constructed and managed by either state or federal agencies. State campgrounds charge a small fee ($1 or $2 nightly). Federal campgrounds charge about the same rates, but also permit access if you hold a current national recreation "passport." This is a credit-card-sized plastic card that you can buy at any ranger station or national park. It's good for a year and currently costs $7.

Aside from reasonable rates, most state or federal campgrounds are located near large tracts of public land. Their setting and layout are always tasteful—plenty of trees and grass and they're often near a lake or stream. The facilities you can depend on here include grill fireplaces, picnic tables, a supply of wood and water, garbage removal, and modern toilets.

Although several heavy-use sites may, most public campgrounds don't include amenities such as stores, showers, electricity, hot water, or laundry service.

UNIMPROVED PUBLIC CAMPGROUNDS are usually scattered around on state or federal land, cost nothing to use, and are a result of the cart following the horse.

Campers themselves establish them by using an attractive streamside meadow or lake shore for a campground; then the Forest Service, conservation department, or some similar agency adds a garbage can. They might eventually install a permanent fireplace and occasionally an outhouse, but aside from that, there will be little improvement beyond the site's natural state.

Unimproved public campgrounds seldom find their way into listings. Finding them is usually a matter of back-road and byway travel. If you're not in any hurry, look for them by all means. You can count on magnificent settings, the smell of pine in the air, and untouched wilderness no more than a few steps from camp.

PRIVATE CAMPGROUNDS amount to nothing more than attractive, potential campsites that are on private land. Never forget that the land is in private hands—not yours via personal ownership or the government's. Always obtain permission before you camp, picnic, or trespass on private lands. Most owners are glad to grant you the privilege if you ask. They'll resent your presence if you don't.

CAMPER'S CHECK LIST

The possibilities for a camper's check list are infinite, simply by virtue of the fact that there are so many different kinds of camping, and so many different reasons why people take a camping trip. A radio and television, for example, may be welcome adjuncts to a mobile home, but they're a little far out if you're planning a week's worth of back-packing. The same kind of contrast holds for items such as mosquito netting, guns, snowshoes, and a portable barbecue grill.

There is, however, a core of equipment that many families have determined as essential for family camping. When reading this list, allow for things like a "tent" meaning any kind of shelter, and a "sleeping bag" meaning any kind of warm bedding (if you're using a motor home, truck camper, or trailer, you'll need neither).

Tent	Cookstove
Sleeping bags	Portable lights
Air mattress or cot	Ice chest
Dining fly (an open	Chairs and folding table
canvas shelter for	Foodstuffs
cooking and eating)	Clothing

Even to the rank novice, the importance of the above items should be clear. The following is a list of things that should also be considered and, we recommend, included in your camping gear.

- Axe, saw, hammer, and nails, for firewood, repairs, etc.
- Leaf rake to clean the camping area
- Spade to dig a runoff for rain, and a safe fireplace
- Broom to clean out the tent or camping trailer
- Food cabinet for protection against animals for stored food

24

- Air pump to inflate mattresses
- Heater, useful if camping trip is planned for early spring or fall
- Water container to keep supply of water at the campsite—this should hold at least 2 gallons
- Pots and pans—at least 3 pots and 1 pan
- Clothesline and clothespins. (Sometimes things get dirty and must be washed.)
- Flashlight for emergencies
- Radio for weather reports, news, recreation
- Tablecloth for a touch of civilization
- Dishcloth and towels, and plastic dishpan
- Can opener
- Eating utensils
- Strong rope—has many uses; can double as a clothesline
- First-aid kit—very important
- Clothing storage—generally suitcases
- Personal grooming supplies
- Recreational equipment, games

Other items of equipment for special uses will come up in later chapters.

If you're like us, you'll soon find that no published "list" is going to answer all your needs. You'll discover some of the items we've included are useless to you, and that we haven't included what you consider important. But one or two overnight camping trips will quickly define for you what you need.

Once you've arrived at your requirements, have a hundred of those lists dittoed or mimeographed. Each time

CAMPING IN COMFORT

you plan and pack, check off equipment as it's laid out. You'll save a lot of time and thought over putting together a list every time you want to camp, and will be sure that nothing will be forgotten.

PLANNING YOUR CLOTHING

If you'll be taking an extended trip, you'll of course want to include clothes you can wear on the kinds of occasions when your camping clothes won't do—dining in a good restaurant, for example.

But what should you take as the day-to-day clothing that will get the most use? It's frighteningly possible to pack six suitcases of this stuff for a family of four "just to be sure." When you're camping, you need space and all those suitcases take up a lot of it—especially when you discover, as we have, that better than half the clothes will go unworn.

The answer we've come up with is something we call "integral garments." It amounts to a wardrobe whose separate pieces are light and cool. When worn in combination, it's warm enough to withstand below-zero weather.

Although you'll undoubtedly come up with variations on the theme, the basic idea goes like this:

You start with standard undergarments—cotton undershirt and pants. Over that, wear insulated underwear. The quilted dacron kind is best. Even in the summer, this is nice stuff to have. It makes excellent pajamas on cool nights.

For basic outer garments, jeans or canvas pants on the

26

bottom, a cotton shirt or a wool shirt for the top. A bulky-knit wool sweater is next, and over that can be worn a tight-weave nylon ski shell. These shells provide no warmth themselves, but they're the best windbreakers made and they're reasonably water-repellent.

Leather footwear of boot design is best for all-around use. Figure on high-topped boots for cool weather, low ankle-cut boots for warm weather. Plan on wearing two pairs of socks under them.

The best headgear is a simple wool skullcap. If you'll be in cool country or doing a lot of work with your hands, figure on one pair of gloves.

Worn all together, this is just about the outfit Sil and I wear when we ski—and that's in temperatures that sometimes are well below zero. Needless to say, you'll be well prepared for any sudden drop in the thermometer.

But unless we get some pretty strange weather changes in the next decade, the average camper is never going to need *that* many clothes. What he does need—and has with that kind of selection—is the freedom to adjust to any conditions by picking and combining the clothes that suit the temperature best. And all from his suit of "integral garments."

If the weather's quite hot, one pair of socks, jeans, and a T-shirt will keep him cool. If he awakes on a frosty morning, high in the Rockies, he'll be plenty warm if he dons insulated underwear, jeans, and a wool shirt. Or he could wear the cotton shirt and a sweater. Or a wool shirt and the ski shell, and so on.

It might also be worthwhile to point out that this kind

27

of clothing selection leaves plenty of room for laundering the clothes that aren't on your back.

BEFORE YOU LOCK YOUR DOOR

You'll have a lot more fun on your vacation trip if you don't have to worry about the home you left behind—and whether it will be there when you get back.

Aside from the obvious details to take care of before you leave—like making sure windows are locked, kitchen garbage disposed of, appliances turned off, newspaper, milk, and mail deliveries suspended—you should also inform the local police of your planned absence and give them a copy of your itinerary. That way, in case of emergency, they can reach you somewhere along the way.

Here are a few other tricks designed to foil burglaries:

- Leave a few old clothes hanging on your washline if you have one.
- Leave a light burning in your living room or bedroom.
- Leave a radio on somewhere in the house.

A light and radio will run you about seven cents a day in electricity, and that amounts to pretty cheap insurance.

2 Hitting the Road

Your wheels, your transportation to, from, and during your camping trip, are more essential to your success and enjoyment than any single piece of camping equipment, yet usually this subject is sadly ignored.

Whether you're a back-packing wilderness wanderer, a boat camper, or the proud owner of a brand-new motor home, you depend on your vehicle to get you where you're going in a minimum amount of time with a maximum amount of comfort and safety.

A great deal of the performance you'll get from your wheels will depend on the condition they're in on the day you leave. Even a new car can give you trouble if you don't include some prepping and planning for both man and machine before you hit the road.

AUTOMOTIVE CHECKUP

Malfunctioning cars are the causes of more camping grief than all the day-long rains, smoky campfires, and burnt beans put together.

CAMPING IN COMFORT

And there's no real reason for most breakdowns to occur. Just about any potential problem can be spotted long before it happens, and either cured or avoided.

Make an appointment with a good, modern garage a week before you plan to leave on your camping trip. We say a week because there's a long chance that you might need some special part or job done, and that takes time.

Tell your mechanic your camping plans—the kind of driving you'll be doing, the climate you'll be in, and how long you'll be gone. Tell him you want your car in top-notch shape for the trip. He should know what to do from there. But just in case he doesn't, and so you can double check on his inspection, here's a list of things that should be looked after.

* MOTOR. Check your points and plugs, and your vehicle's timing. Run a compression test on your cylinders, and inspect the carburetor setting. If you're going to do most of your driving over flat country or at low altitudes without much stop-and-start city stuff, you might want a slightly lean gas mixture. This will save you money on fuel.

GENERAL MAINTENANCE. Change your oil and oil filter, clean or replace the air filter on your carburetor. Get a lube job. Check the fluid levels in your hydraulic systems—power steering, brakes, transmission—and the water in your battery and radiator. If any of these are low, check carefully for signs of leaking, especially around seals.

Generally, all the above-mentioned tasks require a trained mechanic's attention. There are other potential trouble-makers you can check out yourself:

30

TIRES. Flats are a pain in the neck, blowouts are downright dangerous. For cross-country driving, use only brand-name, middle- to top-of-the-mark-quality tires. Don't strike out on a long trip with less than half your tire's original tread. If you do, chances are they will have to be replaced before you get back, and tires don't come at bargain-basement rates in tiny towns. Buy 4-ply tires if you'll be driving a family car or station wagon. If you're using a pickup camper, buy 6-ply truck tires for carrying a medium-sized unit, 8-ply tires if you've got one of the big hang-over-the-bumper jobs.

Beware of the label that reads "4-ply rating." Those tires aren't made with four layers of belting. While this rating game is safe and satisfactory for highway driving, your trip will probably carry you over second-rate roads full of chuckholes or sharp gravel. Highway-rated tires just can't take this kind of punishment for very long.

It's also wise to buy a brand-new spare for your trip. That way if you have a blowout, use your new tire in its stead. If you can't get a reasonable price on a replacement in the first town you hit, you can save some money on secondhand rubber for your spare.

The size of your wheels is important too. For some strange reason, some auto manufacturers see fit to stock their pickups and vans with 14-inch tires. This is ridiculous if you're going to be carrying any kind of load . . . and that's what those vehicles were supposedly designed for.

If you're buying new, insist on 15-inch tires minimum. If you're hauling a heavy load, 16-inch tires are even better. These larger tires mean safety at high speed, less wear on

31

the rubber, better gas mileage, and should you want to get off the road, greater clearance for your undercarriage resulting in more mobility.

FAN BELTS are another common failure. If yours seems the slightest bit feathered around the edges, replace it. Even if all your fan belts are in good shape, it's a good idea to carry extras—and know how to replace them yourself.

WIPER BLADES should be rubbery and "live" to the touch. If they streak your window when it's raining, get them replaced.

LIGHTS. Check out your lighting system: brake lights, directionals, and high- and low-lamp beams, and if any of them are out, buy new bulbs. If you'll be pulling a boat or camping trailer, don't forget that its lights have to be hooked up to your car's electrical system through a socket and plug that are installed in your trunk.

COOLING SYSTEM problems—overheating and boiling over in particular—are right up there with flat tires as the camper's most common automotive headache. Before you leave, have your radiator cleaned and flushed. Make sure that any clinging bugs, grass, or litter is blown out of the cooling fins on the radiator core.

It's also a good idea to install a bug screen across the front of your radiator. This amounts to nothing more than a specially constructed piece of window screening that acts as a shield. It catches any insects or debris that would normally end up in your radiator and prevent the free passage of cooling air.

These bug screens are practically mandatory if you'll be

pulling any kind of trailer. With that extra load, you'll need all the cooling power your radiator is capable of.

SHOCK ABSORBERS should be in good shape for a safe, smooth ride, but if you'll be carrying a heavy load (and most campers do), you might consider replacing your factory-installed shocks with heavy-duty absorbers.

A quick way to find out if this will be necessary is simply to load up your buggy with all your passengers, gear, and/ or trailer. If you notice a significant squat over the rear wheels when you're fully loaded, heavy-duty shocks are for you.

TOOLS. Even if you're no mechanic, it's a good idea to carry a minimum complement of tools. That way, if you do get into trouble, a passing motorist with kindness in his heart and some knowledge about machinery will have something to work with.

Three adjustable crescent wrenches with 4-, 6- and 8-inch handles will tackle most nuts and bolts on your car.

Three screw drivers—one 4-inch standard bit, one 8-inch standard bit, and one 6 inches with a phillips head—will turn any screw you might have loose.

Two pliers, one a combination slip-joint pliers (that's the kind everybody thinks of when you say pliers) and one set of cinch-down-tight-and-hold variety (vise grips) will round out your basic selection of hand tools.

Every car should have a jack and lug wrench, and that jack should be capable of lifting your car when it's loaded with gear. Remember that if you're trailering, your jack should work on the trailer wheels too. Try it out to be sure.

CAMPING IN COMFORT

Occasionally, the stock jacks that come with cars aren't the safest things in the world. Or maybe your car jack doesn't work on your trailer. If you want an extra jack, the safest and strongest we've yet seen is called a Hi-lift jack. They're large and heavy, but they get the job done with ease. Second choice is the screw-type jack that rests on a tripod frame.

And while you're checking out your jack, make sure you've got a lug wrench to fit the nuts on your trailer wheels.

GAS. No matter where you're headed on your camp out, having five extra gallons of gas stored in your trunk is a wise move. You might never need it, but it will pay for itself in peace of mind if you find a gas station you were depending on closed. The safest, most durable, and easy-to-pack cans are the Army-type "jerry cans." They can be bought at most hardware and auto-supply stores. You should also carry a few extra gallons of water and cans of oil.

Surprisingly enough, all these tools, jacks, gas, oil, and water take up very little room—less than an average-size suitcase, if you pack them carefully.

TRAILER CHECKUP

If you're going to be pulling a camping trailer or boat around with you, that piece of equipment deserves a road-worthiness check too. The most important item here is your braking system. If your trailer has no brakes of its own, will your car brakes be sufficient to stop you in a hurry? If your trailer is equipped with brakes of its own, are they working properly?

Get those questions answered by a professional. Because the rest of your trailer amounts to little more than a frame and some wheels, you should be able to do the rest of the inspecting yourself.

TIRES should have at least half their tread and be worn evenly. If they're bare on one side, there's a chance either your wheels or your trailer frame is bent out of kilter. Have them checked over by an expert, and the trouble straightened out. A twisted trailer is an open invitation to hard driving and a potential accident. (This is also a point to consider when buying a secondhand trailer.)

HITCHES. Your trailer hitch (female socket) and car hitch (male ball) should be evenly matched. These balls and sockets come in different sizes. If you've got a 1½-inch ball, make sure the socket is of the same size. A lot of back-and-forth or side-to-side play is a sign they're not.

Cinch the trailer hitch down and make sure it locks in place, that it can't be lifted off.

The trailer must have a safety chain—a fail-safe measure to ensure that, should something malfunction in the hitch, your trailer won't take off on its own. The chain should be securely fastened to the right-hand side of your car bumper. That way if something does let go, the trailer is pulled away from oncoming traffic.

Your car hitch—the ball—should never be one of those bolt-on-the-bumper devices. They're fine if you're pulling a light boat around the block, but they're bound to work loose on a long trip. Instead, have a permanent hitch installed. The best kind to get is the type that stretches its braces well under your car frame and is welded in place.

CAMPING IN COMFORT

It helps equalize the weight of the trailer tongue on all four points of auto suspension.

LIGHTS. Trailer lights are the only rear lights passing motorists will see after dark. Make sure they work. If they don't, you might try burnishing up the male and female electrical hookup with a little emery. Disuse often results in corrosion on the points of contact. This acts like an insulator and prevents passage of the current. If that doesn't work, call an electrician.

LUBRICATION. Your trailer wheels need grease as badly as your car wheels, but often get overlooked. Make sure they have plenty of grease inside. This is particularly true of boat trailers, due to frequent immersion.

MIRRORS. If you'll be driving a truck camper or trailer whose height exceeds that of your rear window, you're going to need special mirrors to get a view of what's behind you. The best kind are adjustable. Get them installed, then with trailer or camper hooked up, set them wide enough to be able to see around your load.

DRIVING WITH A TRAILER

If you and your trailer are brand-new acquaintances, you're in for a few surprises when you first try to back up. It doesn't go where you expect it to. If you don't care for that kind of surprise your first day on the road, plan on a little pre-trip practice.

The best time for that practice is early Sunday morning; the best place, your local supermarket parking lot. Bring a few cardboard boxes or large cans, and lay out an obstacle course. Try to envision a typical campground parking stall or boat-launching ramp, and place your boxes accordingly.

When you back up, the trailer, unlike your car's rear end, goes in the direction opposite to the way you turn your wheel. Here's a detailed explanation of the whole operation.

Begin by pulling forward so vehicle and trailer are in a straight line. Cramp your wheel to the left to start the trailer turning right, or to the right to get it turning left. Straighten out your front wheels as soon as you have the trailer headed in the direction you want it to go.

Backing up for a long distance will require a few corrections, but if you're doing things right, they should be minimal. You should also be backing very slowly.

If you cramp your wheels too hard and fail to straighten out soon enough, your trailer will jackknife—wedge itself into a position where it's being pushed sideways. This isn't good for your hitch, car, or trailer. Never let the angle between car and trailer exceed 45 degrees. If you find you've jackknifed, pull ahead, straighten out, and start all over again.

Driving a trailer when you're going forward is, of course, a lot easier. But never forget that your car is a lot longer than it used to be. Plan on that extra length whenever passing, and don't forget its extra pull should you attempt to pass on a hill.

Pay particular attention to roadside warnings of sharp dips or bumps ahead. If you hit these at high speeds, you're liable to lose control of your vehicle and flip.

When coming down a hill, it's a good rule to do it in

the same gear you used when you started to climb. This saves on your brakes and avoids the possibility of a runaway.

Whenever you're being overtaken or passed by a large truck, a vacuum will be created that will suck your car and trailer toward the truck. This is particularly true when you're pulling a trailer with a lot of side area. Use extra caution in this situation, especially if you're traveling over 40 miles per hour.

Keep your rig to the right at all times. Trailering speeds are always slower than the pace of normal traffic, so extend some road courtesy to those behind you. On a very long hill, you might consider pulling over and parking for a few moments if you see a big line of cars piled up behind you.

PACKING UP

The rules of packing, no matter what or where, are two and simple.

(1) Pack first those items you'll need last. That way, things you need the most will end up on top, within easy reach.

(2) Whenever possible, pack the heaviest items low, the light items high. The reason for this is that like water finding its own level, heavy items will eventually find their way to the lowest, most stable point available to them. If you put them there in the first place, they don't have any potential for getting there under their own steam—crashing, crunching, and breaking, or causing sudden, unsafe weight shifts.

We might include one other packing rule here too. Make

sure everything fits before your planned departure. It's a little frustrating to be "all packed up and ready to go"—with a hundred pounds of gear still sitting in your driveway and no place to put it.

Although these rules are constants, they do have slightly different applications in camper, car-trunk, and trailered-boat situations, so let's take a look at each.

CAR TRUNKS are perpetually designed with one persistent fault: as soon as you fill them up, you can't get to your spare. That's one reason why it's wise to place all bulky, heavy items in there: suitcases, coolers, campstoves, and large tents. Then, if you have to unload them in a hurry, you won't have to move a lot of small items that usually are of the variety that soil easily. The trunk is also one of the lowest points on your car, and low weight makes your car handle better than high weight. Which brings us to the subject of . . .

ROOF RACKS, boxes for extra storage space mounted on the roof of your car, are a boon to the camper, providing storage space for stuff that would normally clog up the available passenger room. But they should be used wisely.

Place the rack well forward on your roof and load it up only with light gear: sleeping bags, pillows, air mattresses, and aluminum camp chairs. Racks are rated for a safe load at between 200 and 300 pounds, but you're smart to keep it closer to 100. When you turn a sharp corner, all that weight up top exerts a sizable amount of tug, and it makes it a little tougher to drive.

Some roof racks are sold with canvas covers; others are open to the elements. It's a good idea to cover your gear with a canvas tarp if it's exposed. Make sure air can't get under it from the front, and hold it in place with rubber tie downs. These can usually be bought in sports and hardware stores.

CAMPER TRAILERS AND PICKUP CAMPERS have a packing rule in common. Stow all heavy stuff low, and make sure it's well lashed down or locked in place. That's particularly important for the contents of refrigerators and cabinets.

I learned the value of that rule about ten years ago on one of my first experiences with a camper.

A buddy of mine had just bought his first camper trailer and was aching to try it out. It being fall, we decided to take a run down to the Salmon River Canyon and hunt chukars, an exotic partridge imported to this country from India and well established in that area of Idaho.

Foolishly, we crammed our grub, cooking and eating gear, shotguns and shells, into any available space: on top of bunks, on dinette seats and tables, and on the sink counter. We closed the door on our gear and my Brittany Spaniel, Duchess.

The road to Idaho goes over Lost Trail Pass—a twisty, winding cowpath that drops down from the high country in a hurry. We were both eager to do some hunting, so maybe Bill was a bit too heavy on the gas pedal instead of the brakes.

When we got to our destination, only a few miles beyond the bottom of the Pass, we parked the car and opened the camper door.

The floor was a mishmash of grub, dishes, pots, pans, shotguns, and shells. Duchess wasn't around.

40

We finally found her on the top bunk, cowering in the corner, afraid as much from the flying saucers as from the fact that she knew she wasn't supposed to be up there.

Since then, she's been a bit reluctant to ride in a camper or trailer, and when I leave her there, she always casts a wary eye toward high storage spots. Of course, now I do too.

Although lashing down or locking in cabinets everything that might move is common to all trailers and truck campers, the distribution of a load isn't.

A truck camper should have most of its weight forward, snuggled close to the cab of the truck. This is so the load will be equally balanced on all four wheels.

On a trailer, weight should be distributed around the unit fairly evenly. Tongue weight—the pressure put on your car's trailer hitch—is the consideration here. All trailer hitches are designed to exert a specific pressure on your ball (a figure usually included in the trailer's specifications), and that weight should not be altered by more than 100 pounds when your trailer is loaded. Careful distribution of gear—not too far forward, which adds weight, not too far back, which decreases it—will keep the tongue weight within range and prevent trailering problems (usually excessive sway). While it's hard for most humans to judge a 10- or 15-pound weight difference, 100 pounds either way is easy to feel by simply lifting the trailer tongue by hand before and after you load.

BOATS ON TRAILERS lend themselves to the same rules governing travel trailers, but what you place where should be even more carefully judged. A boat is supported on a trailer

41

at points of contact that distribute any weight strain evenly around the hull. If you concentrate too much weight in one spot, you run the risk of upsetting that delicate balance. Your boat then develops a bulge resulting in poor performance, or a leak which might mean no performance at all.

ON-THE-ROAD DRIVING TIPS

Getting from your home to your campground can mean a trip of several days. You'll find the drive infinitely more pleasurable and safe if you pace your driving by taking frequent rest stops and never trying to cover too many miles in a day. Plan on switching drivers *before* the driver is desperate to rest—at least at every gas stop.

When you're under way, make sure everyone buckles up his safety belts and double locks his door. An ounce of prevention, you know.

Safety should always come first, but savings are pretty close to any camper's heart, particularly when money is involved. You can save quite a bit on gas if you find a comfortable speed, and stay there. It should be somewhere in the 50-to-60-miles-per-hour range. Speeds in excess of 60 miles burn up an excessive amount of gas.

Avoid fast, floor-boarding starts and sudden stops. Both actions use tire rubber and gasoline.

Make frequent checks on your tire pressure too. Tires should be at the manufacturer's suggested pressure first thing in the morning when they're cool and haven't been used for several hours. If you're driving them under improper pressure, they not only burn up gas, they burn themselves up too, through excessive wear.

Sunglasses go a long way toward more comfortable driving. They cut not only the glare of the sun, but the glare from your nice, shiny hood. Should you begin to feel uncomfortable in the driver's seat, try moving your seat forward or backward. It will change the strain on the muscles in your back. A pillow, either under you or low against your back, achieves the same effect.

Perhaps one final word is useful about speed limits when you're on the road. Obey them religiously, particularly when passing through small towns. Although the practice is on the wane, there still are a few places with a police force who support themselves by the tickets they collect. Needless to say, this kind of setup results in overly rigorous law enforcement. And it's tough to fight city hall—especially when you don't have the time.

OFF-THE-ROAD DRIVING

If your dream is finding a campsite on some back road or byway with no one to bother you, where the trout will bite a bare hook and wild animals are your only company, you're going to have to tackle some pretty tough terrain. Here are a few tips on how to do it—and stay out of trouble.

You're going to have to begin by increasing your complement of tools. In addition to your jack, lug wrench, spare gas, water, oil, repair tools, shovel, and axe, you'll want to carry a tow rope or cable, tire chains, a 2-foot-long hunk of 8-by-10-inch board, and a tire pressure gauge.

Each situation you might get into requires slightly different techniques to get out, so let's take a look at your potential problems one by one.

CAMPING IN COMFORT

MUD is a common curse to the guy behind the wheel. Unless you're sporting four-wheel drive, you'd be wise to avoid any travel over country you know to be greasy, gooey gumbo. Of course, there always is the chance that you'll get a heavy rain while camped deep in the hinterlands. If that happens to you, and you can't wait until the country dries up, chain up immediately.

As you're driving along through mud, even with chains, your rear end is going to want to catch up with your front end. Don't let it. Keep correcting to hold your wheels in a straight line. If you come to what looks like a particularly bad spot and you've got to cross it, hit it at top safe speed. Don't try to inch across a mud hole; you'll never make it.

Should you get stuck, break out your jack, mount it on top of that 2-foot chunk of wood (without that support, you'll jack the base down instead of the car up), and jack each rear wheel clear of the hole. If you're really in, like up to the frame, you'll have to do the same in front. Fill the holes in with sticks, rocks, any kind of solid substance available. Next, lay a solid path of sticks or rocks along the route your tires will take. Make it wide because you're bound to fishtail a bit.

Once you get moving, don't stop until you're well clear of the trouble spot.

ROCKY ROADS require a gentle touch. Ditto for deeply rutted roads. The trick here is to avoid any collisions between rocks and the soft underbelly of your car, and to do that, you'll have to drive very slowly. Inch up and over heavy boulders and let yourself down easy by playing the brake pedal. On rutted roads, drive far to one side of the road.

This is called "driving the crown" and takes advantage of the high mounds of dirt or gravel pushed out of the way when the ruts were made.

If you're hearing a lot of scraping and grinding, you might consider lightening your load and raising your clearance by having all your passengers get out and walk for a while.

SAND is loose-consistency stuff. The reason people get stuck in it is because their tires cut down into it rather than float on top of it. To increase your car's floatability, reduce your tire pressure so your tires balloon out. A pressure gauge is useful here. Eight to ten pounds of tire pressure is usually standard.

You might also remember that wet sand holds together much better than dry sand. This means driving will be easier after a rain, or if you're on an ocean beach, close to the water. Don't get too close though, and by all means don't get stuck for too long. Oceans have things called tides.

If you do happen to get bogged down, the procedure for getting out is exactly the same as the one for mud. And don't forget to pump your tires up at the first gas station you see once you're back on good pavement.

SNOW isn't a problem usually associated with camping, but it's a lot more common than most people think in the Rocky Mountain West. In our home town of Bozeman, Montana, weather records show snowfall on every day of the year (not all in the same year, however). And your chances for running into snow increase with your camp out's proximity to spring and fall.

45

CAMPING IN COMFORT

Should you run into snow and aren't sporting snow tires, either pitch a camp or put on chains. You're asking for trouble if you try to tackle this stuff with smooth tires.

Momentum is the biggest thing you've got going for you here. Get moving, and keep moving. Don't floorboard your car or try a sudden stop. You'll break traction and go into a skid.

If you're stuck despite chains, chances are it's because there's a big pile of snow under your car, cradling it and keeping weight needed for traction off your rear wheels. Break out your shovel, and clear your undercarriage. You should then have enough go to get unstuck.

TROUBLESHOOTING

There are giveaway signs that a driver is heading for mechanical trouble. If you take note of them and act accordingly, you'll, at the very least, keep your repair bill and the time spent on repairs to a minimum.

Establish a habit of watching the GAUGES on your dash, and glance at them immediately if you begin to hear unfamiliar sounds in your engine. Your *oil gauge* measures the amount of pressure behind the oil that's lubricating the engine. If there's no pressure, the oil doesn't get to moving parts and friction burns up your engine. If your oil gauge reads below low, or your red dash light flashes, turn off your engine and check your oil. If you're low, add some oil from the cans in your trunk. Recheck the level and look for signs of leakage at the next gas station you see. If you find plenty of oil in your engine, and your pressure stays low, see a mechanic in a hurry . . . and don't drive there.

Temperature gauges measure how hot your engine is. When you're pulling a trailer on a long hill, or when your cooling system is dirty, your engine can get hot enough to boil your coolant away. (This is especially common at high altitudes where boiling points are lower than at sea level.) If your gauge reads hot, stop your car and slowly remove your radiator cap. If water's been lost, wait a few minutes, then add some water with the engine running. If there's plenty of water in there and it's gurgling and boiling away, plan on waiting a half hour or so for your engine to cool down. Then get your cooling system and fan-belt adjustment checked in the next town.

Your *ammeter* reads the level of electrical charge being produced by your generator (or alternator). If the needle rides squarely in the middle of the gauge, all is well. If it swings to "discharge" or rides high on the "charge" side, you might have electrical problems. Cars lacking the needle gauge will signal trouble by a red dash light. In either case, get it checked by a mechanic. (Again, it might be nothing more than a loose fan belt.)

Another sign of trouble is excessive sway while you're driving. It either feels as if your rear end is sliding around or as if you're driving a snake. This usually means you've got a low tire on your auto or trailer. Stop right then and check it out. Chances are that if you are getting a flat, it's a minor puncture that can be easily fixed. If you ride on it for very long, you'll have to buy a whole new tire.

Should you have a complete breakdown and need help, a universally recognized signal for assistance is an open hood with a slip of white cloth tied to your door handle or radio antenna.

47

3 Back to Basics

Many campers and outdoorsmen with a few years' practice under their belts tend to belittle books of instructions. But a first grader has to learn the alphabet before he can gain experience in reading, and a camper has to have the same kind of primary education before he can live comfortably and properly in the outdoors.

By getting back to basics, you can build your camping experiences on a strong foundation. There is nothing more rudimentary than selecting the foundation for your camp—the campsite.

CHOOSING THE CAMPSITE

If you've planned your itinerary in detail, chances are you know just where you expect to camp, but the best-laid plans of mice and campers can go awry. A public campground you picked might be filled to capacity. Private lands you remembered to be open last year might turn up posted. Maybe you just don't like the site of the commercial campground you planned to use. Whatever the reason, you suddenly have to find another spot.

Your primary consideration should still be what kind of camping and recreation you want. Is there some favorite trout stream you wanted to fish, a historical site you wanted to see? Perhaps you're just passing through on the way to another place, and had planned to use this stop to take in a movie and do some backlogged laundry. What *you* want to do will determine where you'll want to locate your camp, and again you have the choice of four options.

The first possibility is that you'll want to find a commercial campsite.

COMMERCIAL CAMPGROUNDS can be most quickly located with a telephone. Just find a booth and consult the Yellow Pages. If you have trouble tracking down the possibilities in a phone book, call up the local chamber of commerce which should be listed under the town's name: for example, Phillipsburg Chamber of Commerce. If you're too late and they're closed, try a few gas stations or the local constabulary.

When you get a phone number or two, call the campgrounds before you get back in your car. They just might be full. If they're not, they'll be glad to reserve a space for you.

IMPROVED PUBLIC CAMPGROUNDS don't offer this phone-call convenience, either in finding their location or obtaining reservations. Your best bet here is to thumb through a copy of Woodall's *Trailer and Camping Guide,* or Rand Mc-Nally's *Guidebook to Campgrounds.* Find the public sites available and start making the rounds. You'll usually find those campgrounds with the least facilities filled last, so if finding a place for the night looks tight, shoot for them first.

When setting up shop in either improved public camp-sites or commercial operations, try to locate yourself near conveniences. Walking a hundred yards with a bucket of water or armful of wood is good exercise, but it isn't much fun. Make sure too that you're not about to park yourself in a depression that will collect water after a shower. If you like a fire at night, see that your chosen spot has a place for one. (Most regular campsites prohibit fires outside of fireplaces.) Picnic tables at a site are another invaluable convenience.

UNIMPROVED PUBLIC CAMPGROUNDS AND PRIVATE LANDS. Although there is much to be said for commercial and state campgrounds with their conveniences, central location, and opportunities to meet with other campers, many people feel that something of camping is lost when you step into a new morning and are greeted with a tent and camper city. If you want the challenge of camping in unspoiled nature, you have to pay a special price: a price of time spent looking for a site, a price paid in extra work, such as carrying water, chopping your own wood, and living more primitively than if you had chosen a constructed campsite. You also have the responsibility of finding a safe spot for you and your family. But in a big way, the price is part of the satisfaction you get, and many campers are more than willing to undertake it.

Unimproved campsites, on either public or private land, are sometimes hard to find on the spur of the moment, particularly in the crowded East. The best place to begin is with a road map. Most of these oil company giveaways mark not only primary and secondary roads, but little-traveled country roads, trails, mountain ranges, rivers, streams, and lakes. They'll at least give you a clue as to what that section of the country offers exploring campers.

Any place that's easy to get to and looks appealing will usually be taken early in the day, so stay off main roads and travel little-used byways that wander off into the woods.

If you find an attractive site on private land, track the owner down and ask permission to use his land. He'll give you the go-ahead if he's reasonably sure his land won't be defaced or littered.

Once you've found a satisfactory spot, you can get to work pitching camp, but don't forget the precise placing of your campsite is just as important as the general location. The difference of a few feet is frequently the difference between fighting the outdoors and enjoying it.

The first consideration when searching for an isolated campsite is water; the amount is up to you. If you want to fish, swim, or boat, you'll need a lot, but if you're just interested in camping, a tiny trickle for drinking and cooking will do. In this day of people and pollution, you can never be sure that a source of water is uncontaminated, so if you'll be camping on your own, carry decontamination pills, available in Army surplus stores, drugstores and some sporting goods outlets. If you can't find them or if you forget them, boiling the water for 15 minutes will eliminate harmful bacteria, as will 3 drops of iodine per gallon of water.

51

CAMPING IN COMFORT

Certainly not all water is polluted, and if you've camped in an unpopulated area where the water is clear and cold, well filtered, and aerated by rocks, chances are the water's safe to drink. Natural springs that bubble up from the ground are particularly safe, and if you're used to chlorinated water, they'll pleasantly surprise you with their fresh, clean taste.

Look next for a reasonable margin of safety. Never park yourself close to a cliff or extremely steep hill, especially in the spring and fall. Frost action will loosen rocks and they could come roaring through the campsite during the first hour of sunlight. If you suspect this situation to exist, look around the site before you set up. If you notice freshly broken, newly arrived rocks around, find a different location.

Hollows and the bottoms of gullies and gulches look like great places to pitch a tent, but avoid them like the plague. Hollows are ideal for filling up with water during a heavy shower, and usually are well supplied with mosquitoes. Small gullies are there as a result of water drainage, and if a rainstorm comes by, your campsite could well have the questionable advantage of running water—right through the middle of your tent.

Water, and where it will drain in the event of rain, is always an important consideration, particularly around your tent or pickup. When making your camp, look for a spot that has natural drainage. A small rise is ideal, but not always available. A very gentle hillside is also quite good, but don't forget that you'll have to dig a small ditch on the uphill side of your tent or trailer to guide rain water away from your sleeping and eating area.

A spot with low grass, away from tall trees, is particularly desirable, because grass will hold back water and drain it into the earth. Grass feels great underfoot too, and better yet under your body if you happen to be sleeping on the ground.

"I think that I shall never see A poem lovely as a tree" are the first two lines of a poem by Joyce Kilmer, and if you've ever camped in an area where there aren't any trees, you'll know what he meant. Trees are as much a part of camping as any tent or campfire. But beware of large trees, particularly during thunderstorm season. A tree with a trunk 6 inches thick or less is usually young enough to bend with the wind and short enough to avoid lightning, yet will provide shade, protection, a handy clothesline, and a feeling of being in the outdoors.

If your location checks out so far, you're ready to set up camp in safety. Here are a few other points to look for that will make it comfortable as well.

Make sure that you're not too close to dense grass, swamps, or thick brush. Tall grass is a fire hazard, and swamps and brush nearby will have you slapping at mosquitoes and no-see-ums before the sun goes down. If your campsite is subject to light breezes, so much the better, since it will keep flying insects of all varieties from taking to the air.

Light breezes that freshen the air and cool the evenings are pleasant companions to camping, but don't let yourself in for a future windstorm that will blow half your camp away. Big lakes and deep canyons are frequently subjected to high winds, so if your campsite is near one, get close to a windbreak of medium-sized trees, or tie your tent down well.

Beach campers can plan on quite a bit of wind and little protection, so if you're pitching your camp on an ocean shore, make sure that anything used to anchor equipment to the soft sand has a wide flange on it. Special sand spikes are made for this purpose. A wide, thin board or piece of driftwood will work in a pinch, provided you drive it deeply.

Another problem the sea affords that doesn't present itself to inlanders is tide. Make sure that your camp is far above the high-tide mark. The sound and smell of surf are wonderful sleep-inducers, but catching a wave in your lap at three in the morning isn't the best way in the world to wake up.

Just as the evening breeze provides welcome relief from the heat of the day, you'll want the sun to cut through the cool of the early morning. Face your camp to the east and the morning sun. Since the winds in this hemisphere prevail from the west, this will also keep your shelter entrance and fire downwind in normal weather.

If you're driving a trailer or pickup camper, all you've got to do is park. If tenting or sleeping under the stars is your idea of camping, sweep the area thoroughly. Sticks, stones, and pine cones can puncture tent floors, air mattresses, and ruin a night's sleep. If you haven't brought a rake or a broom, a heavily needled bough or a bunch of limber twigs will do the job.

PLACING YOUR CAMPFIRE. Although fires and men have known each other for a long time, it's always been a touchy partnership. Men have learned that a friendly fire can quickly become a devastating enemy if it gets out of hand. When working with fire, remember your ABC's: Always Be Careful.

Fires should never be built on open ground. It's hard to keep them contained, and therefore quite dangerous. Commercial or public campsites provide pre-constructed fireplaces, designed to avoid fire danger, but if you're camped in an isolated spot, it's up to you to build a safe fire. Here's how it's done:

Should you be camping in the vast national forests of the West, or on large tracts of unbroken woods anywhere, obtain a fire permit from Forest Service or state personnel first. These permits cost nothing and are used only to determine the location of a controlled fire. If you forget to pick one up, you're likely to find an army of smoke-jumpers parachuting into your camp. This can be an embarrassing experience for anyone.

Select the fireplace location carefully. It should be at least 10 feet from any burnable object, and well away from overhanging limbs and branches. Dead tree stumps, roots, and peaty soil pose a hidden danger. Fire can "go underground" in this stuff, smolder for weeks, then gradually work toward the surface and start a new fire.

Rake the immediate fire area clear of any leaves or branches to ensure that flame won't creep beyond the fireplace.

Next check the prevailing winds. Make sure that the area you've selected for a fireplace isn't subject to sharp gusts of wind that could carry a wayward spark into your tent or the woods.

CAMPING IN COMFORT

Many of the fundamental truths of camping are contained in a set of postulates we call Fineagle's Laws. The particular law that involves campfires reads: "No matter where you locate a campfire, you'll be directly in the path of smoke." The corollary to this hypothesis is, "When you move, so will the smoke." These rules were written to illustrate some of the problems of camping, and we've found they have a ring of truth. Nothing is so maddening or stifling as sitting in a constant pall of smoke, and the stuff does seem to search you out. You can cut that contact to a minimum, however, if you'll locate your fireplace downwind of tables, chairs, work areas, and sleeping quarters.

Once you've found a safe place for your fire, dig a shallow hole and pile the dirt you remove around the edge. That pile of dirt is an excellent emergency fire extinguisher, and should eventually be used to bury the dead ash before you break camp. (It will also fill up your hole and leave your campsite just as you found it.)

Next, build a wall of rocks around your fireplace at least 6 inches high. The best rocks to use are those of the magmatic variety—rocks that were originally cast from molten lava, rather than being pressed into shape. These volcanic rocks resist cracking and chipping in the heat of the fire, and provide a more stable, safe base for cooking or looking. The worst rocks for fires are slates and shales. Don't use them unless you have no choice.

Most purposes can be served best by a fireplace about 2 feet in diameter. A larger fire than this gets too hot to get near, and tough to control. No matter what size the fire, you should keep a full bucket of water and a shovel nearby for that very necessary margin of safety.

FIRES FOR COOKING, LOOKING, AND COMPANIONSHIP

There are many kinds of fires and their designs are called "lays." Each lay has a job that it does best.

THE KEYHOLE LAY is the best all-around choice for camp cooking over a fire. It incorporates both the tipi fire and the log cabin fire, providing light, cooking, and warming heat all at once. Dig a trench and hole in the shape of a keyhole, and surround it with rocks. In the round part of the keyhole, build a tipi fire. You've got light and heat.

As the tipi fire burns on, scrape the coals into the trench part of the keyhole. That's your cooking fire.

If you're in a hurry, you can build a log cabin fire in the trench, establish a quick bed of coals, then use the tipi fire to replenish your supply.

TIPI FIRES are built by standing lengths of wood upright and arranging them in a conical shape like an Indian tipi. They provide lots of light and, because the flames lick at the top of the structure, high-level heat for warming bodies. This is the best choice if you're interested in a fire to share an evening with.

LOG CABIN FIRES provide fast, even heat and a quick supply of cooking coals. They're best built in a square trench in the ground 18 by 24 inches on a side.

The wood is laid down flat in a loose crosshatch pattern containing three or four layers. Because there's plenty of room for air circulation, they're easy to get going, and burn up all the fuel at once.

57

Keyhole Fire

Tipi Fire

Log Cabin Fire

THE REFLECTOR FIRE. If you're a quickie camper or back-packer, here's a warming fire that will heat the inside of a lean-to. Dig a slit trench 3 or 4 feet from the front of your lean-to, and build up the far side of the trench with a wall of rocks. Lay a log cabin fire, but build it tilted against the wall of rocks. The rocks will reflect and concentrate the fire's heat toward you. You can make this fire even more efficient if you first surface your rock wall with aluminum foil.

THE SQUAW FIRE deserves mention only because it's not the thing to do. It amounts to throwing an armful of wood over a starter fire in a haphazard fashion. Indians called this a squaw fire because it was inefficient and useless, and usually the kind built by men who didn't know any better—men comparable to "squaws" in their estimation. Squaw fires are unpredictable. The way they burn is determined by the way the wood falls. On one extreme they can burn slow and smoky. On the other extreme, they'll ignite quickly and burn hot and fast. The rapidly settling wood and flying ash can be a fire hazard.

STARTING THE FIRE

It isn't always easy to start a fire, particularly if the wood is damp or wet. Here are a few tips that should help you start a campfire in any weather.

If you aren't too limited in what you can carry, always bring along some newspaper, wax paper, or better yet, a commercial firestarter for your initial flame. The best gadget we've ever seen for fire starting is an impregnated ball of waxy "starter tape." You cut off what you need as you want it. The wax content in the tape burns with a heat that quickly dries out even the wettest twigs.

If you haven't any of these items, try toilet paper or paper towels. When you're really in a bind, pine cones have a resin content that's quite flammable. Ditto pine needles, and especially the pure resin that drips down the side of pine trunk wounds like candlewax.

If the woods are wet, look for abandoned bird and squirrel nests. These nests are always built in a rainproof spot, and their insides will be dry and tindery.

Next, collect tiny twigs. They should run no larger than pencil thickness. If you can find stuff thin as a toothpick, so much the better. You'll find the driest branches prickling out from the trunks of large trees. The larger limbs of these trees act like an umbrella in the wettest weather. If a branch snaps crisply when you break it, it's dry. If it twists and is hard to break in two, forget it and look for a drier piece.

Once you've collected your tinder and kindling, lay down two sticks about 2 inches in diameter in the middle of your fireplace. Space them 4 inches apart. In the center of the two sticks, place your paper, nest material, or whatever tinder you're using. On top of that, lay a fistful of twigs in a loose crosshatch pattern.

Strike a match, and your fire should start.

When your kindling catches, avoid dumping a whole armful of fuel on top of the flame. Instead, carefully add slightly larger and larger pieces of twig as the fire grows. Once the base of the fire contains some glowing coals, you can begin to add heavier wood.

YOUR WOOD SUPPLY

The performance and function of your campfire aren't determined only by the structure of your fireplace. The wood you use has a lot to do with them too.

The species of wood you use isn't as important as some people think. In the case of a night or warming fire, all you're interested in is flame, and any dry wood will burn. When you're cooking you should be using coals only, and again, any kind of wood will produce coals.

Size is, however, important. Wood for cooking coals should be no thicker than your wrist, no thinner than an inch in diameter. Smaller wood burns too fast and goes directly from flame to ash. Log-sized wood doesn't work well either; the outside will be coals while the inside is still unburned wood. This produces yellow flame, which you don't want.

Any wood for coals should, of course, be thoroughly dry. If the bark has fallen off, so much the better.

When you want a warming or light-producing fire like the tipi lay, choose wood up to 3 inches thick. Wood any bigger than that won't burn with a bright flame unless you have a real rip-roaring fire, and safety dictates that you don't want one of those.

If for some reason, you want a holding fire—a low-flame, cool affair that burns on without much attention or addition of wood—you can use logs up to 6 inches thick. Any logs bigger than that are a bit foolish. They take a lot of work to cut, and then must be split for any kind of performance.

61

CAMPING IN COMFORT

And while we're on the subject of cutting, here are a few tips for the camp lumberjack. An axe around camp is highly overrated as an efficient woodcutter. They're fine for sharpening and driving stakes, and clearing brush, but hacking away at a huge log for firewood is a colossal waste of energy —and potentially dangerous.

A collapsible campsaw—a thin-bladed bowsaw (also called a swedesaw) that folds into its own handle—is far more practical for large cutting jobs. Use this whenever you can't get through a hunk of wood with two or three swipes of an axe.

If wood is thin enough to break over your knee, do it that way rather than chopping or sawing. Again, you'll be saving energy and be safer too.

CAMPFIRE COOKING

The most essential piece of cooking equipment for the campfire chef is a grate. Nothing intricate—just a simple grate with folding legs that can be poked into the ground. You can also use an oven, barbecue, or refrigerator grate laid over a rock fireplace.

By poking the legs deep or shallow, or removing or adding rocks, you can get the food close to or far away from the heat source. It's a little like turning the heat up or down on a kitchen range.

Grates weigh little, pack flat, and eliminate more headaches than any other single piece of cooking equipment. But a word of caution; if you have a brand-new grate and plan to use it as a grill with raw food placed directly on it, scorch it well before using it. Many of these grates (particularly refrigerator shelves) are covered with a protective metallic coating that must be burned off before you use them. Otherwise food will taste strange.

If a grate cuts 30 per cent of camp cooking headaches, always cooking over a good bed of coals will eliminate another 40 per cent. One of the most obvious signs of a dude camper is a pile of black pots with a roaring blaze underneath. The bright yellow flame you first get when you build a fire is fine for light, but bad for cooking. It's too hot, too erratic, and will turn utensils as black as coal. Wait for the fire to burn down, at least until the wood is covered with white ash and small flames hang over the logs. You'll burn less food, spend less time cleaning up afterwards, and turn out a much better meal.

The cooking procedure is a lot like that in your kitchen. Heat cooks food no matter if it comes from electric coils or campfire coals. Although you can't adjust the precise amount of heat under your meal, you can maintain fairly even cooking conditions by using a few tricks.

Besides the aforementioned raising and lowering of the grate, you can add more coals from your tipi fire to get more heat. If too much heat is the problem, sprinkle a little dirt on the fire and it will cool down. (You can use water instead, but use it in tiny amounts.)

Pay lots of attention to what's happening inside your pots and pans. If you're frying foods, and the grease is hot and spattery, move your pan to the side of the grate, away from the main thrust of heat. Cool the fire down, then gradually move the pan back toward the hot spot until the crackling meets with your approval.

CAMPING IN COMFORT

The heat of your coals doesn't make much difference when you're boiling foods—you're cooking just so long as you hear the pot bubbling. But remember that at high altitudes, boiling temperatures are lowered. You'll have to compensate for that lower temperature by cooking things longer. This goes for steamed and baked foods too.

Here are a few facts that might help you figure your cooking time in the high country. Boiling temperature at sea level is 212 degrees F. At 10,000 feet, it's down to 194 degrees F.

At a mile high, a 3-minute egg takes about 5 minutes. Cakes require more water and baking time than the recipe calls for at sea level, and a stew that takes 2 hours to cook on an ocean beach would take a little over 2½ hours in the mountains.

Also remember that liquids will boil away faster too, so you might have to add some extra water before your potatoes will be done.

Foil cooking is a real blessing to the campfire cook too. It involves nothing more than wrapping food (fish, chicken, baked potatoes, etc.) in aluminum foil, then burying the foil in a bed of coals. It not only tastes good—there are no dirty pots or pans to do after your meal.

A few other work-, time-, and blister-saving hints for the camp cook include:

• When you're cooking canned goods, open the top and heat them right in the can. There's no reason to dirty extra pots.

• "People who play with fire get burned" states one of Fineagle's Laws, but you can avoid many blisters by wear-

64

ing gloves when cooking, and using long-handled utensils. It's surprising how far heat will reach up the handle of a frying pan, so the longer the handle, the better.

• A vital part of comfortable camping is the avoidance of unnecessary work, and there is no more abhorrent and useless task than scrubbing lampblack from the backs of innumerable pots and pans in a chilly stream. Even with good coals, you will get a little lampblack, so to solve this problem, line the outside of your pots with aluminum foil, then after the cooking and camping are done, throw away the foil.

If you're using a very hot fire, foil will sometimes burn up. A paste of laundry soap and water, spread liberally on the outside of the pot, will make the soot come off much more easily when you have finished cooking. You can do this with or without a foil covering. If you have neither soap nor foil, some good gumbo mud will have the same effect, as long as you don't mind chipping your pots clean instead of washing them.

No matter what type of fire you build, gather plenty of wood for it—enough for the evening fire so you won't be stumbling around the woods looking for more fuel after dark, and enough so you can set aside some dry kindling for the next morning's fire. Dew alone can soak kindling thoroughly, and an evening shower can make a fire for the morning's coffee troublesome. Cover a small pile of wood the night before if you want a fire first thing in the morning.

Campers realize many benefits from a campfire, but with the benefits are responsibilities, because the minute a match is struck there is the danger of a forest fire. Never leave a campfire unattended. It takes a few short minutes to start a holocaust that could burn for weeks. When you're through with a fire, drown it dead out with water, then shovel dirt over the fire bed. If you smoke, crush your butts and matches well, then grind them into the soil with your heel. If the woods are unusually dry, use fire as little as possible. It might be a slight inconvenience, but it's a cheap insurance on the outdoors for future generations.

CAMPING MANNERS

One of the many bonuses that camping offers its participants is the feeling of friendship and camaraderie between campers. The same bond that makes boatmen wave at each other on the open seas and moves mountain climbers to lend aid and assistance to anyone in trouble exists among campers.

Although simple survival isn't as pressing a problem as it once was, this notion of interdependence is present in many ways. If you ever have a flat on a car towing a camp trailer, chances are a camper will stop to give you a hand. If you ever run out of some important commodity, and a fellow camper has an extra supply, he'll be only too glad to lend it to you.

It's a comforting feeling to know that you can depend on your neighbor, but as a camper, you have the responsibility to return the favor, and there's no better place to start than in the practice of good camping manners.

In a crowded campsite, one of the most frequent breaches of etiquette, and the most disturbing to others, is the practice of getting up early and loud. Early rising is all right in itself, but early risers who make a lot of noise are bound to lose friends. Many people camp to relax, and that relaxation includes plenty of undisturbed sleep.

Everybody forgets things—it's only human—and other campers are more than willing to lend you food, gas, matches, or whatever you need with no questions asked. But don't forget that by accepting their gracious good will, you make a contract, unwritten but binding, to return those supplies as quickly as possible. If that's impossible, offer to pay for them. Because camping usually includes some degree of isolation, supplying each other with necessities is a great convenience that shouldn't be taken for granted.

All people need privacy, and in a crowded campground, that's pretty hard to find at times. It's an accepted rule that the area inside the guy wires of a tent belongs to the guy who owns the canvas. In less crowded campgrounds, figure that the site itself—fireplace, picnic table, parking stall, etc. —is under your neighbor's temporary domain. Don't park your gear on his picnic table or barge by the door of his camper on your way to get a bucket of water.

Camping is enjoyment for everyone, including the kids. Every age group can find something in camping to interest them. The five-year-old can learn the intricacies of an earthworm or a mole tunnel. The ten-year-old can climb a tree, and the fifteen-year-old can take off on his own and go fishing. Kids enjoy camping, but all campers don't enjoy kids.

Children have a magic way of getting into, around, and under things that spell trouble and inconvenience for others. So keep them in reasonable tow if there are other campers in the vicinity. The camper on the next site might be getting away from his kids for a week end and if so, it's a sure bet that he doesn't feel like being confronted with yours in the meanwhile.

If wandering children can sometimes be pests to others, wandering pets can double the discomfort. We hate to see a dog chained up, but if you're in a crowded campsite, it's a real necessity, as well as the rule in most campgrounds. We've seen dogs steal a family's meal from a picnic table, and worse yet, urinate on a box of food. They can soil a campsite so thoroughly that everyone had better keep shoes on. Even if your dog is better behaved than that, the mere sight of a drooling cocker spaniel as you sit down to supper amounts to an unnerving experience if he's not your own. So keep your dog over by *your* tent.

Another problem that has arisen with the advent of mass camping is the disposal of waste. Campgrounds used day after day for an entire season can accumulate a fantastic amount of human discards, resulting in an unsightly mess and odor. Even the most innocuous-appearing liquids, when accumulated in enough quantity, can become offensive.

The most important consideration is, of course, solid waste material. It should be put into a garbage can. Since most people know that wastepaper, cans, and foodstuffs should be thrown into a receptacle, there's no problem with this kind of garbage. The real problem in heavily trafficked campsites arises with the disposal of liquid wastes. Most people assume that dishwater, stale beer, curdled milk, and the like will simply sink into the soil. This works fine, until it's done day after day after day. Then the soil simply can't handle all the foreign material, and grass dies, shrubs die, and an odor results.

The best method of liquid disposal if no sinks or drains are available is to dig a shallow hole. Dump all liquids in it, then close the hole when you leave. This at least gets them down into the subsurface soil, where they're less likely to do damage.

Liquids can damage soil, but they can devastate water. Never dump liquid wastes into a lake or stream. It takes a very small percentage of this stuff to kill fish and aquatic life.

If outhouses are provided, you're expected to use them—never the great outdoors.

Building fires in some campsites can offer one problem. Even where fireplaces are provided, wood sometimes isn't, and the immediate area is usually picked pretty clean.

If this is the case, the first place to look for your wood is on surrounding trees. Even if the ground is totally swept clean, there are usually attached dead branches that remain overlooked. But remember, break those branches clean at the trunk, particularly if they're close to eye level. The sharp remains of a branch can easily put an eye out or open a nasty wound if unnoticed by a wood picker.

Experienced campers know that green wood is useless for most fires, but some beginners don't. Never cut growing branches or trees. This is not only wasted work, it's downright destruction. It takes many years to grow a tree and one axe stroke to destroy it. If even a small percentage of campers were this thoughtless, most campgrounds would be barren wastelands in a year. Heavily used areas have laws that prohibit the cutting of live trees and you could be in for a fine by this thoughtless action as well. In the campgrounds where wood is supplied, don't hoard it; leave enough to go around. Deliveries are usually made every day, so take enough for a twenty-four-hour period of use and no more. Wood-hoarding will not only make you unpopular with other campers; it will make you unpopular with the camp manager who has planned on how much his patrons will use and is supplying wood accordingly.

WILDERNESS CAMPING MANNERS. If you're fortunate enough to get away from the crowds and into a wilderness campsite, you won't have to mind your camping P's and Q's quite so much. You can make all the noise each other can stand, and let the kids have a free rein to explore and wander about at will. But you'll have a bigger responsibility in the long run.

Unestablished campgrounds are not policed; they have no garbage service, no outhouses, and no one will come along after you leave to pick up that scrap of paper or tin can that you didn't notice. It's your responsibility to leave the campsite looking as if no one had been there before, and it requires a little more work.

Beyond fire safety, the most important consideration is the disposal of waste. Pour liquids into a hole, and burn any and all combustibles. At one time, a garbage pit was sufficient for disposal of cans and bottles, but not any more. Conservationists and Forest Service personnel alike plead with campers to take away any nonburnable wastes and put them in the first garbage can they see. Aluminum cans and bottles never decompose; animals will dig up a garbage dump as soon as it's abandoned; and even in true wilderness areas, the traffic is getting so heavy that garbage pits and their telltale signs are getting as thick as craters on the moon.

Of course if it's physically impossible to take away the garbage and cans, a pit is better than leaving them around. Dig it deep, at least 3 feet, and 4 is better. Thoroughly scorch all cans and bottles. This not only eliminates food odors; it helps decompose the metals. When you bury your garbage, throw some ash in with it for the same reason.

You will probably have to construct a makeshift toilet too. Again, dig a deep hole and use it exclusively. Try to locate it far away from what could conceivably be a campsite in the future, and if you're going to be there for a length of time, frequently sprinkle lime in the hole. Build the latrine downwind from the campsite, and when you leave, fill in the hole and any other holes or ditches you might have dug, tamping the earth hard.

A good rule to follow in any campsite is to leave the site looking a little better than the way you found it. This custom got its start with the cowboys and mountain men who would leave some food in a stranger's cabin they had used. It was a gesture of thanks, as well as a useful means of paying rent. It also ensured that future travelers, perhaps caught short, would have something to eat during their stay. A clean campsite means that future campers will have pleasant surroundings when they want to stop by your old spot.

C. B. Colby, the camping editor of *Outdoor Life* magazine, says all these things in a few short words. He calls them his "Ten Commandments of Camping," and they're sage advice indeed.

CAMPING IN COMFORT

(1) Thou shalt not arrive or depart a campground with great chaos.

(2) Thou shalt not despoil any living thing about thee.

(3) Thou shalt not be slovenly about thy tent site.

(4) Thou shalt not make loud noises after 10 P.M.

(5) Thou shalt not let thy pets and children run wild.

(6) Thou shalt not give advice unless it is sought after.

(7) Thou shalt not hesitate to give aid if it's needed.

(8) Thou shalt not crowd thy neighbor unduly.

(9) Thou shalt not borrow unless it be desperate.

(10) Thou shalt not know more about camping than all others.

SAFETY AROUND CAMP

More than one trip has been ruined by a lost child. You can solve half your apprehensions about letting your children run free to discover the wonders of the outdoor world if you'll buy them all a whistle. Require them to have it with them at all times. Sometimes the best way to accomplish this is to pin the whistle to the inside of their clothing, but don't hang it around their neck. This practice could spell tragedy when they climb trees, or serious injury when they are running through the brush. If they do happen to get lost, all they have to do is blow their whistle, and you can hear them two miles away on a calm day.

Although you may like to get a suntan and you dress accordingly, young children usually don't care about it; so dress them in long clothing and boots and you'll spend less time dressing scratches, insect bites, poison plant blisters, and abrasions.

Boots are a good idea for the entire family too, especially for anyone who is chopping wood, or does a fair amount of hiking. A good pair of boots won't blister your feet, they provide extra protection against bruises and sprains, and if fitted correctly, are amazingly comfortable for walking. For most camping situations, high-top leather boots are the best. If you do a lot of camping in hot weather, you might consider the low ankle-cut variety.

ANIMALS. Association with nature and wild animals is part of the camper's reward, but campers and their children should never make the association with wild animals too close. Even a little chipmunk can inflict a painful bite, and the bigger the animal, the bigger the potential danger.

People who fancy themselves as outdoorsmen and have read a few chapters of *Bambi* assume that deer are gentle animals who flee at the first sight of man. While this is usually the case, there are always exceptions. Female deer have razor-sharp hoofs, and can kick an intruder severely. Bucks have deadly horns that can gore, maim, and kill.

If you're in the real wilderness, moose should be avoided at all costs. They're as big as a locomotive, and nasty as a shrew. Bears, even the mighty grizzly, usually steer clear of this tough customer. If you're threatened, throw your dignity aside and climb a tree. But pick a big one, because if he's mad enough, he'll try to knock it down.

Many people are naturally wary of bears, and it's a fine idea, yet there are verified cases of tourists in Yellowstone Park putting their children on the back of a bear to take a picture. This is sheer idiocy, for a bear could kill a child, or man for that matter, with one swipe of his powerful

73

paw. No matter how "tame" any wild animal seems to be, steer clear of him; he's as dangerous as dynamite with a lighted fuse. This is particularly true of young animals, who seem safe enough until you realize that the female parent is probably close by. If she senses danger, she'll come thundering down to protect her offspring the only way she knows how: with horn, hoof, or claw. Wild animals are children of nature, but not toys. Watch them at a safe distance.

CAMPING'S COMMON DANGERS. Serious injury is seldom the result of such natural circumstances as animals, landslides, and violent storms. It's usually the camper who's his own worst enemy. Nine-tenths of camp accidents can be laid at the door of the individual who pushes himself beyond his limitations, fails to take necessary precautions, or misuses his equipment.

Cuts from knives and axes occur because the handler loses control of his tool. It may surprise you to know that a razor-sharp cutting edge is safer than a dull one. Dull tools tend to glance off a surface because there's no edge to get a good bite, and the direction of the axe or knife stroke is then out of control. If you're careful how and where you cut, the stroke will be spent on air, but that unfortunately isn't always the case. Cuts from dull instruments are usually jagged and hard to close, too. It pays in work saved and injuries avoided to keep all cutting edges sharp. And, of course, when axes and knives are out of use, always keep them sheathed.

During the camping season, papers frequently carry a story about some hapless outdoorsman who burned himself seriously, blew up his trailer, or started a forest fire when he tried to light a gasoline stove. These stoves and heaters are wonderful comforts, but they can become terrible instruments of destruction if not handled properly. Gasoline evaporates quickly and fills the air with fumes. The fumes from gasoline, once mixed with air, will burn and explode. Any activity with gasoline should be done in the outdoors, where the fumes can disperse quickly. If you spill some gas on the ground, or on the stove, give it ample time to dry before you strike a match, and make sure that you haven't splashed gasoline on your clothing.

There's a particular danger involved with white gas— the fuel most commonly used for campstoves and heaters. It has no "gassy" odor, and is as clear as water. The only safe way to store this stuff is in a red metal can with "gas" plainly marked on it.

Never use gasoline to start a fire; gas is so potent that it explodes and burns in a few seconds. The explosion is dangerous, and the length of burning time usually not enough to get a fire going.

A fire extinguisher should always be part of a sportsman's traveling gear. You may never use it, but it's a godsend when it's needed. Extinguishers are important to have not only while camping, but while traveling as well. An overheated engine and a leaky fuel line can spell the end of your car through fire—a fire that water can't put out. But a commercial extinguisher can quickly control gas or electrical fires, and save you a whale of a lot of money and time for a relatively small investment. A practical place to store an extinguisher is under the front seat of your car or camper.

Fire means heat and comfort, but no matter how cold

you are, never use an open flame of any kind in a sealed area unless it is vented in some way. This includes every kind of heat but electric. Even the modern catalytic heaters that work by chemical process rather than combustion use up oxygen. Open flames produce heat—and carbon monoxide as a by-product. Carbon monoxide is a deadly poisonous gas. The only place where an open flame is relatively safe is in a canvas tent, since the material allows quite a bit of air passage through the pores in the cloth. If you're in any kind of weather-sealed structure, use a catalytic heater and open a window a crack, or make sure your stove has some sort of chimney.

If there's one lesson that a few days' camping will teach anyone, it's neatness. A cluttered campsite is impossible to live with or work in, particularly after dark, and there's no better time to straighten up scattered belongings than right before supper. It's not only more pleasant to have neat surroundings, but at night it's a lot safer.

Although statistics show that most accidents occur in the immediate camping area, there are a few things to remember if you strike off on a family hike or decide to find that hidden lake where the trout are a foot long.

Never go on extended hikes alone. If something does happen, you'll need someone to go for help. If a real challenge presents itself—like scaling a rock cliff or walking across a gorge on a narrow tree—don't accept it. Just the fact that you view it as a challenge indicates you're unsure about whether you can do it or not. The price you might have to pay isn't worth it.

But personal danger isn't always so easy to identify as a

possible fall from a rocky cliff. It may take far more subtle forms.

Overexertion results in more injury to campers than any other single cause. You can't suddenly jump from a desk job into a vigorous outdoor life. If you huff and puff going up hill, or cutting wood, you're out of shape, sure. But so are 90 per cent of the adult males in the United States. Sit down and let your breath catch up with you. By pushing yourself beyond your ability, you could push yourself 6 feet under. Know your physical limitations and cater to them.

First aid. Cuts, burns, and insect bites are an expected and accepted part of outdoor living. Even the most conscientious outdoorsman will occasionally touch a red-hot panhandle, or slip with a sharp knife while carving. But the smart camper foresees these accidents, and carries a first-aid kit to ease the expected pains and minimize injuries.

First-aid kits should be neat, compact, and housed in one box set aside exclusively for that purpose. Because we do a lot of boating, our favorite is a small Navy surplus kit, made of metal with a waterproof rubber seal. We removed the ancient contents and restocked it with fresh supplies.

If you don't want the bother of gathering your gear from drugstore shelves, you can buy a complete prepacked first-aid kit from Johnson and Johnson.

As important as the kit is a first-aid book that will tell you what to do for common injuries as well as remotely possible emergencies. The Red Cross publishes a basic one, and there are others, equally inexpensive, that are usually

77

available in drugstores and bookshops. Any of these books will contain a check list of suggested contents for your first-aid kit.

One item in your kit is sure to be adhesive bandages—Band-Aids or the like. In addition to their more obvious uses, these are invaluable for small temporary repairs around the campsite: a small rip in a tent wall, a puncture in a poncho, or even a tear in a pair of waders.

And of course in addition to the contents of your kit, there are other things you should have with you that have to do with physical protection and comfort. Sunglasses are invaluable—not only for the glare of driving, but on beaches, in snow, or in high mountains. Insect repellent—both for area spraying and for application to exposed parts of your skin—is a must.

The best treatment for insect bites is, of course, prevention. In addition to the use of commercial repellents, you can protect yourself by wearing long clothes in the early morning and in the evening, when insects are most likely to be out. For bites or stings, there are a variety of remedies—and as many theories about what works best—and your best bet is to consult your own doctor on this at some time before you go camping.

Knowing a few things about insect types might help you avoid an unfortunate run-in.

• Stinging insects—wasps, bees, hornets, and yellow jackets—inflict the most painful bites. Remember that unless you somehow disturb their nest or hive, they want absolutely nothing to do with you. Even if a bee or wasp swings menacingly over your head, chances are he's just curious. Leave him alone. If you start to see a lot of these

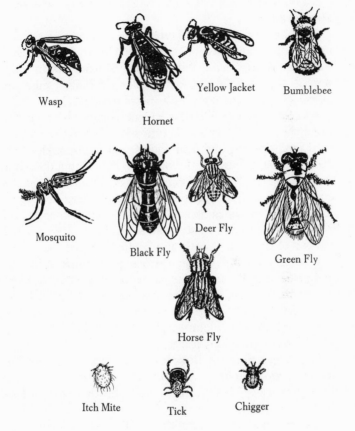

Wasp

Hornet

Yellow Jacket

Bumblebee

Mosquito

Black Fly

Deer Fly

Green Fly

Horse Fly

Itch Mite

Tick

Chigger

insects, or if you get stung out of the clear blue—get moving. You haven't noticed it, but they've set up housekeeping very nearby.

• Biting insects—black flies, green flies, horseflies, and most notably mosquitoes—are attracted to you by your body warmth. When these pests are in evidence, wear long-sleeved shirts and dull, neutral-color clothing. Douse exposed parts of your body with insect repellent.

• Creepy-crawlies like ticks, chiggers, and itch mites burrow into your skin and itch furiously. To keep them out, wear long clothing and dust your sleeves, cuffs, ankles, and neck with sulfur powder. If you find a tick in you, douse his tail with lighter fluid or kerosene and he'll pull his head out on his own. If *you* pull him free, chances are he'll leave his head in, and open a chance for infection. Chiggers and itch mites that have made a home in you can be evicted by way of an alcohol bath around the infected area.

• Poisonous plants are another campside cause of itching and scratching. Poison ivy, sumac, and oak are the common culprits. Poison ivy is the most widespread of the three. It usually twists and climbs around fence posts and deciduous trees, and can be identified by its three-leaf cluster of smooth-surfaced, pointy leaves.

Poison oak also has three-leaved clusters of oak-looking leaves. It grows in low bushes or shrubs, and is less common than poison ivy. It's usually found only in the southern half of the nation.

Poison sumac is the toughest of all three to identify. It has the same finger-like leaves of ordinary sumac, but the edge of the leaf is smooth rather than saw-toothed. Poison

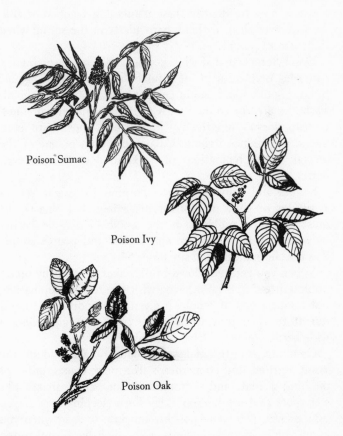

Poison Sumac

Poison Ivy

Poison Oak

sumac has white berries—berries of the non-poisonous kind are red.

Know how to identify these plants and teach your children to steer clear of them, particularly in the spring when they're most potent.

Don't forget that their "poison" can be carried on a pants leg or the fur of an animal that has rubbed against them. Should you come in contact with a poisonous plant, wash the area of contact with a strong soap several times. If soap doesn't nip the ivy in the bud, most burn ointments will reduce itching. Calamine lotion, or one of the several other preparations of its kind, does the job even better.

Snakes and things that go bump in the night get an awful lot of copy in outdoor magazines, but they're the most overrated problem in the woods. Do-or-die battles between scorpions, spiders, and snakes and people simply don't occur in a camping situation.

When you get right down to it, snakes are actually pretty noble critters who raise havoc with the rodent population, but want no part of people. If given the opportunity, they'll retreat to their own world every time. Just give them a wide berth, and you'll have no trouble.

Camping country and snake country are seldom the same. Rattlers and copperheads like rocky places, unfit for pitching a tent, and cottonmouth and coral snakes like wet spots that are far too soggy for a sleeping bag. If you hike or fish, you could possibly run into one, so when you know you're in snake country, wear high boots and watch where you put your hands.

If the unusual does happen, and you get bitten, it's important to keep calm and immobilized. The slower your heart beats, the less damage the venom will do. Your first-aid book should contain advice on emergency treatment, but the main thing is to get medical help as soon as possible.

Still, we feel safe in saying that you'll never run into a poisonous snake because they're just as interested in avoiding you as you are in avoiding them. In fifteen years of camping, hunting, fishing, and hiking, we've seen exactly one rattler. And our dog was at the bottom of that.

FINDING YOUR WAY in the woods is important savvy for any outdoorsman. Each season sees hundreds of campers, hikers, and fishermen getting lost, and consequently tying up thousands of men and dollars in rescue attempts. Like all camping accidents, getting lost can be easily avoided by a little forethought and hindsight: forethought in planning your trip into the wilderness, and hindsight in remembering where you've been.

When you plan a trip far away from civilization, use a map. Have a good idea of where you're going, and tell someone else about it. If your trip will take you into a national forest, stop off at a district ranger station and let a ranger know of your plans (and pick up a fire permit too).

If you're going on a hike for a day—a side trip from your base camp—use a map to locate the direction of your goal and its relation to your campsite.

Carry a compass with you. As you're walking, remember prominent landmarks such as mountains, cliffs, or odd-looking trees, and always be aware of where you are in relation to the sun. Every ten minutes, stop and try to find the direction of your camp through the lay of the land, the sun, or your compass. After a few hours of this, remembering direction becomes second nature, and you'll have no trouble finding your way back.

But circumstances do arise where all the information and instruction in the world can't help. Compasses can be lost, and fog can hide mountains and sun. If this ever happens, and you have told someone where you'll be and when you'll be back, sit tight and light a fire. Three of anything in outdoor language means "help needed": three rifle shots, three signal flares, or three blasts on a whistle. Just remember to sit tight, and don't panic.

Alternatively, if you're in good shape and in a relatively small patch of wilderness, you can get out by yourself by remembering to follow water. This eliminates the chance of walking around in circles, and since civilization usually locates near streams, you will eventually get to a farmhouse or village. But remember, you could be letting yourself in for a 24-hour journey, so if you have some doubts about your capabilities, conserve your energy and wait. You'll be found.

Dog troubles. People seldom see snakes, but dogs have a knack for searching them out and getting bitten. A dog can find a snake through his sense of smell, corner him, and be in real trouble. If you know you're in snake country, keep your dog tied up. You'll save both of you a lot of worry.

Dogs can add a lot to a camping trip, but there will be times that try the most patient souls. One of them is when the family pet mixes it up with a skunk or porcupine. Some dogs only do it once and learn not to try it again, but there are others who never seem to learn. There are antidotes for both problems.

The worst skunk odor can be eliminated by a good vinegar or tomato juice bath. Vinegar doesn't really smell much better than the skunk, but disappears in a shorter time. The dog won't think much of either idea, so if you have a big dog, you might need help.

If your dog comes whimpering into camp with porcupine quills all over him, you've got a battle on your hands, but you can make it a short one by snipping off the very tip of the protruding quills, then bathing what's left in vinegar. This softens the quill, and it can be pulled out a bit more easily than if it were dry. Always pull quills with pliers, and be firm and fast. It hurts the dog, but it'll hurt him a lot more if the quills stay in.

No matter what problem could conceivably arise around camp, from your dog to your campsite, you can eliminate it or avoid it by planning and precaution. Many beginners seem to think that safe, comfortable outdoor living comes only after many months of suffering and endurance. This is a ridiculous notion. Successful living in the outdoors can be managed quickly. It is based on two things: a knowledge of what to expect, and most important, good common sense.

PETTY THIEVERY

It's an unfortunate fact of camping life that thievery of equipment is on the rise. At one time, a camper's site was his castle, and no one bothered it or the equipment placed there. You can't count on that mutual respect any more though, so if you frequent crowded campgrounds, it pays to take some preventive measures.

Place identifying marks on all your equipment. Two identification marks are best. One should be a very noticeable symbol—your initials, a special color paint on the equipment, or paint scratched off in a prominent spot. This will discourage someone from picking gear up on whim since it's so easy to spot.

Make your other mark hidden—a small number in an unnoticed corner, or a dot of red paint on the inside of a hasp. This makes identification easy should the thief do a paint job over your larger marks.

When you're leaving large equipment around the campsite and you'll be gone for a while, chain it all together and lock the chain. It's fairly obvious to other campers that something's wrong if a guy is dragging a chained-together train of camping gear towards his car.

Keep all small articles out of sight, inside your tent or car. Very expensive items, such as cameras and guns, should be under lock and key at all times, either in your trunk, glove compartment, or under your car seat, out of sight.

It's also a good idea to inform neighboring campers of any planned, extended absences. They'll be glad to keep an eye on your tent and equipment, and you can return the favor when they want to take a trip for a day.

4 Quickie Camping

Each year sees more and more people becoming campers. In Wisconsin, Michigan, and New York, they line ribbons of black asphalt on Friday afternoons, headed for their favorite campgrounds like migratory birds.

Even in the low-population states of Wyoming, Montana, and Idaho, vacation-bound truck campers and trailers are prominent throughout the summer months, doubling and sometimes tripling the normal flow of residential traffic.

Tourist meccas like Yellowstone and Yosemite are crowded. Bumper-to-bumper traffic is everywhere, and campgrounds there are filled to capacity by 11 A.M. every summer's day.

One solution to the crowded conditions of summer camping is simply not to go then. Plan your vacation for the months of June or September, and the number of fellow campers vying for a chunk of the great outdoors will be cut by three fourths.

Another solution is to become a quickie camper.

Quickie camping has quite a bit going for it. Your equipment is at a minimum; it's streamlined and functional. Mid-summer, the time best suited to the quickie camper, is warm and predictable. There's no real need for a large canvas home, heaters, or even the evening warmth of a campfire.

This means increased flexibility and independence, opening up an unlimited number of campsite possibilities for you. Because your camp takes up little space and needs few facilities, your "campground" can be a vacant lot, a bulge in the shoulder of a country road, or even a small city park. Your camp can be pitched and struck in ten minutes or less, so this is also the way to go when you're interested in eating up the miles and saving money on motel bills.

"Quickie camping" didn't exactly start that way with us. It sort of evolved as a natural counterpart to wilderness wandering and horse-packing. When you learn how to carry an efficient, comfortable home on your back, doing the same in a car trunk is a snap.

It works the other way too. Should you someday find your eyes fixed on a rugged mountain peak, on a canoe and wilderness waterway, or on a bike trail leading out into the desert, much of the equipment and many of the techniques applicable to the quickie camping you've done by car will easily adapt to your carless venture.

STATION-WAGON CAMPING

A station wagon is the best investment for the quickie camper. Bed is no further than your back seat, your tailgate doubles as an instant table and eating area, and packing your gear is a breeze.

The most important asset in comfortable station-wagon camping is a mattress. Both fiber and air mattresses are available commercially, and some of them even have contoured sides to allow for the bulge of your car's rear wheels. We recommend air mattresses rather than fiber for two reasons. First, if you need extra storage space, air mattresses can be deflated and folded away. Second, in the warm, stifling nights common to the South and Midwest, sleeping outside is a real pleasure when compared to the hot, close interior of a car. Fiber mattresses get dirty easily, and unless used with a ground cloth, will absorb moisture from the earth. Air mattresses provide a natural moisture barrier since they're essentially rubber, and they can be washed clean when they get dirty.

A wise addition to station-wagon camping gear is a plywood sleeping platform. This gadget is usually constructed to sit 12 inches or so above the floor of your wagon. You can build it yourself by using ¾-inch plyboard.

Support it with legs on all four corners and one leg in the middle. This platform allows for plenty of storage space underneath which means you won't have to spend a lot of time making your bed in the evening, then finding a place to put your gear every time you make or break camp. You can just leave your bed set up in the rear.

In the summer, you'll undoubtedly want a few windows open for air circulation. You can bet you'll get a few bugs circulating too, unless you buy cloth screening (available at some sports and hardware stores and through any tent and awning company). Cut squares that fit a space a little larger than the window that will be open. You can tape your screen temporarily in place, or, if you're worried about the finish of your car, you can lock it between the top of the door and the roof, and add a few snap clothespins on the bottom to keep the screen from wafting in evening breezes.

If you prefer, you can buy screens specially made for your car. They are available for most popular makes of automobiles.

Screens are pleasant in the summer. In fall and spring, a source of heat is even more welcome. One of the nicest things about wagons is that they're relatively well insulated, and don't take much to keep warm. You might consider one of the small (3,000 to 5,000 BTU) catalytic heaters now on the market. They'll run all night on one filling of fuel and will keep you toasty.

Never forget the danger of heaters eating up all the oxygen in your car. Crack a side window about an inch and you'll be safe. *Never* use an open flame heater in an enclosure that isn't vented.

Privacy is sometimes hard to find when you're station-wagon camping, since you could very well "camp out" in a supermarket parking lot or superhighway. You might consider curtains on the windows. Aside from privacy, they also cut the glare of the morning sun so you can "sleep in" after a late night on the road.

TENTS FOR THE STATION WAGON. Back-deck sleeping is essentially a venture for two. If you're a family man with pint-sized campers, or like to travel with a lot of friends, there are tents made specifically for use with a station wagon. The simplest kind is nothing more than a zip-up canvas cover that closes in the rear end when the tailgate and rear window are in the open position. This means you can leave the rear seat in place, and bed down two tiny campers—one in the front and one in the rear seat—while you and your wife sleep in the back.

Still more room can be had by using a roof-mounted tent that unwinds into sleeping accommodations for two. It's carried on racks and is no bigger than a roof-top gear box. Prices on this kind of extra bedroom run $50 to $100.

If you like adjoining bedrooms, many of the major tentmakers have standard models that have been altered to zip up to the rear of a station wagon. The most practical one for quickie camping we've seen yet is the Thermos Pop Tent, with the station-wagon fly. While there are bigger and roomier tent extensions on the market, this one goes up in a hurry, and to our way of thinking, that's the prime consideration in quickie camping.

Station-wagon "campers" deserve mention if only because they're not the thing to buy. They're a solid-walled home, designed to fit on the roof and droop down over the tailgate of a wagon. Their cost is close to an economy-line truck camper, and after you fix up your wagon to take the weight strain (shocks, overload springs, heavy-duty tires, and they still perform poorly), you've got the same kind of investment as a medium-priced camper unit.

THE WAGON MODEL BEST FOR CAMPING. All auto manufacturers turn out an assortment of wagons for a dozen different uses. Assuming your wagon is going to have to double as a family car when not on vacation duty, here are a few things to look for when buying.

• Four doors. Two-door models might seem economical

CAMPING IN COMFORT

in price, but you'll soon cuss the inconvenience of reaching over the back seat or climbing over the tailgate every time you need equipment.

• Head space. You'll be much happier camping if you can sit up straight in the back without bumping your head. Don't forget to include the height of any sleeping platform you might plan to build.

• Motor. Economy of performance is of course a consideration, but we've learned the hard way to steer clear of six cylinders. A small V-8 gives good gas mileage and acceptable performance and power.

• Suspension. Far too many wagons come with stock springs and shocks. No matter what you're using your wagon for, chances are it will often be toting a heavy load. Make sure the one you buy is equipped for an overload.

To supplement wagon space, consider adding a tiny trailer: A small, one-wheeled utility trailer will have no effect on ease of driving and will serve a dozen useful purposes. With one of these trailers, you can leave your bed and daily needs (stove, cooler, camp kitchen) set up in the back of the wagon, and keep occasional items (extra clothing, fishing and hunting gear) stored. This cuts packing and unpacking time by more than half.

TARPS AND TENTS FOR THE QUICKIE CAMPER

If you don't own a station wagon, you can still enjoy the advantages of quickie camping, but you'll have to make arrangements to sleep outside your vehicle.

Shelters that lend themselves well to a nomadic outdoor life should be just that—shelters. When you camp for a

Lean-to

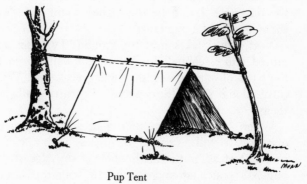

Pup Tent

week, poles, guys, tent pegs, and the time spent pitching a canvas cottage aren't much of a problem. But one-night stops require quick erection and take-down.

Simplicity is the companion of speed, and one of the simplest methods of shelter is the canvas or plastic tarp.

At least for this kind of job, we both lean to plastic. It's light, durable, and compact. We also prefer clear to black plastic, as much for heat avoidance as aesthetics. The best size for this purpose is 8 by 10 feet.

There are two basic shelters that can easily be put up with a tarp: the lean-to and the pup tent. Both of them are most quickly pitched the same way: with rope and clothespins.

Stretch a rope between two trees (clothesline and parachute cord both work well). If one tree is a slender sapling, so much the better. Bend it a bit before you tie down and you won't develop any slack in the rope. This rope is then the ridgepole. It can be the highest point on a lean-to or the ridgepole of a pup tent.

Next, drive stakes into the ground. Two feet apart has proved sturdy enough for us. If you want to go through the work of cutting and sharpening pegs, fine. We usually carry along some thirty-penny carpentry nails and use them.

When tying the tarp to the pegs, don't puncture the material; it will tear and be useless with the first light breeze. Instead, put a small pebble in the edge of the cloth, bunch a pouch around it, and tie your rope around the outside of the pouch. If you really want to be sophisticated, you can buy adhesive-tape tie downs that perform the same job, or an ingenious device called a Visklamp.

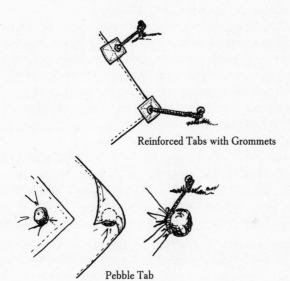

Reinforced Tabs with Grommets

Pebble Tab

Visklamp

CAMPING IN COMFORT

When using a lean-to, fold the end of the plastic material over several times, and attach it to your rope ridgepole with spring-loaded clothespins. On a pup tent, snapping clothespins along the top helps keep the material from bunching up on your ridgepole.

Even if you don't want to bother with pitching these elementary rain shelters for yourself, any camper should carry the fixings for them, and know how to do it. They have plenty of other uses. You can throw the plastic over your gear during a sudden shower, make extra storage space for cluttery items in a permanent camp, and build a play area for the kids on a rainy day.

If you don't want to go through the work of figuring things like tie-down spacing for yourself, plastic tarps are now premade for camping. They have built-in reinforced tabs and grommets, and come in bright, cheery colors. If you have trouble locating these items in a standard sports store, try a shop that caters to mountaineers and skiers.

PREFABRICATED TENTS for the camper in a hurry are the same kind that are suitable for wilderness travel. They're light in weight, and made of tight-weave nylon or poplin cloth. They should be able to be pitched in a hurry, and when taken down, should fit into a breadbox-sized package —poles, pegs, and all.

If you have more than a passing interest in getting off the beaten path and into places that auto campers never see, buy the good mountain tents for your quickie camping. They should be light (3 to 5 pounds, with poles) and incorporate a sewn-in floor and zip-up entrance. Two-man tents are around 5 by 7 feet, and this is sufficient to accommodate two adult sleepers and a nominal amount of gear.

Although there are many designs of mountain tents on the market, when it comes to economy of weight and space provided, few styles can beat the modified wall tent. This unit has a peaked roof sloping to perpendicular walls about 6 to 12 inches high. You'll find your mountain tent a lot more enjoyable if you have enough headroom to sit up straight in it, so make sure your choice incorporates this feature. Costs on this quality gear don't exactly amount to a bargain basement sale; prices start around $60.

If the unusual lightness of the mountain tent doesn't strike you as an advantage, and you could use more space than sleeping for two, you might consider the pop-up tents that have come into vogue in the past few years.

These canvas shelters can be erected in minutes. The job amounts to plugging fiberglass supporting rods into the proper places and "popping" the tent into an erect position in much the same way as you open an umbrella. Sleeping accommodations in one of these amount to room for a family of four, or three adults. It costs about $85. There is a smaller model on the market suitable for one adult or two children that sells in the $50 range.

SLEEPING BAGS AND MATTRESSES

A good night's sleep, or lack of it, is probably the most reliable test of the success of any camping trip, and here we write particularly to husbands.

When I first introduced Sil to camping, she loved the days of sun, the abundant green, the fishing, and the hik-

97

ing, and equally dreaded the nights. They almost cooled her on camping permanently.

She simply couldn't get a good, solid eight hours of sleep, and it was largely my fault.

Way back then, money was in pretty short supply all the way around and we made do with some skimpy equipment, sleeping bags in particular. Then, too, I just couldn't imagine any kind of outdoorsman who wouldn't sleep on the ground, and figured outdoorswomen should sleep the same way.

Well, since then I've learned a few things under her tutelage, and must admit that I was simply young and foolish. Now, whenever we want to sleep under canvas or the stars, our portable bedroom boasts quite a few comforts—and we sleep like babes.

FILLS. Sleeping bags are made a bit like a quilt that zips into a cocoon. The outer layer is usually a tight-weave cotton, specially treated to be moisture-resistant. The inner layer is flannel. Between the two is an insulating material that does the job of keeping you warm; this is called fill.

All new bags are required by law to carry a little tag listing what their fill consists of. Don't buy a bag with wool, cotton, or kapok fill. All three types will absorb moisture from your body and the ground, and they mat as well, flattening out after a few nights' use. The fluffy pockets of trapped air keep you warm in a sleeping bag. Matted, damp fill will get you cold in a hurry.

The synthetic fibers—most notably Dacron Fiberfill—are the most practical fills for the average camper. They attract and hold a minimum amount of moisture, and retain their resilience after many years of use. Three to four pounds of this stuff inside your bag will provide plenty of warmth for May-to-September camping. If you'll be outdoors in the late fall and early spring, you might want to use a bag with 6 pounds of the stuff.

Down sleeping bags, with a fill of waterfowl down, are undeniably the best on the market. Their advantages include lightness and compactness; a 4-pound down bag will keep you as warm as an 8-pound Dacron bag, and press into a package a quarter of its size. But down doesn't come cheap. Figure $25 for each pound of down's worth of sleeping bag.

CONSTRUCTION. Sleeping bags come in two basic styles: the standard square bag and the mummy case. Like down versus Dacron, the mummy case is excellent under specialized conditions, but most campers find its form-fitting contours too confining. The square bag gives you some room to move around so sleeping in it comes closer to the bed you left at home.

Two other variations on the theme are the double bag and the children's bag. The double bag is either designed to accommodate two sleepers from the start, or can be made by zipping two single bags together. (Not all bags will do this; manufacturers will state when it can be done with mated bags.) We're all for romance, but frankly, the double bag doesn't make it in the outdoors. At least twice a night, the two occupants decide to roll in opposite ways at the same time and the sleepers find themselves snubbed up like a roped calf, their covering drawn tight as a banjo string. Even in more compatible positions, there's always

99

a little opening in the top of the sleeping bag between the two warm bodies, and the cold night air whistles between them.

Children's bags, on the other hand, are quite practical. They contain the same ratio of fill as their large counterparts, but because there's less material used, they're a bit less expensive. Then, too, a child's body heat doesn't have to work double-time to warm the unused portion of the bag—he stays warmer and gets a better night's sleep as a result.

When choosing your bag, make sure to select one with a full zipper (when unzipped, your bag will stretch out like a large blanket). Sleeping bags should be aired and dried out frequently. Full zippers make the job a lot easier.

Several companies are now offering a bag that has a zipper on both sides. If you camp in warm weather only, this is a wise choice. By unzipping both sides, you can keep a little cooler on hot nights. If you do any cold camping, they're not too advisable; no matter how well constructed your bag might be, there's quite a bit of heat transfer through a zipper.

Camping equipment was once exclusively olive—and drab—but bright new colors now spark up the campgrounds. Buy a bag with an attractive design on the inside; it's not only pleasant to the eye, it doesn't show dirt quite so much as a solid color. The outside of the bag, however, should be selected with dirt, ash, and grass stains in mind. That's what it will come up against.

And speaking of the outside, bags with fully waterproofed coverings aren't as good as they might seem at first glance. True, the rubberized material keeps water out, but it also keeps your body moisture in. Even treated halves aren't all that good. They offer problems when you want to dry-clean your sleeping bag, which, incidentally, shouldn't be done too often.

You'll prolong the life of your sleeping bag if you clean it by airing it out on a line, then beating it gently when it's bone-dry. To keep it really clean during use, buy a sleeping bag liner and slide it inside. When it gets dirty, take it out and launder it. It will pay for itself in the avoidance of dry-cleaning bills and a longer life for your bag.

AIR MATTRESSES are as essential to a good night's sleep as a top-flight bag. They cushion you as gently as a feather bed, and put an insulating layer of air between you and the ground.

The cheapest air mattresses are nothing more than mattress-like beach toys. They do have a place in that they're light and roll up into a small bundle, but they puncture easily and are slippery as ice. You'll slide off one ten times a night unless you shove it into the lower pocket on the outside of your sleeping bag, and even then it occasionally pops out.

Somewhat better and more rugged are the rubberized fabric air mattresses. These sleeping pads can endure quite a bit of punishment, but have one drawback: their compartments are usually long, round tubes, so the entire affair has a roundish feel to it. You tend to roll off them often.

The best sleeping pad by far that we've come across is a square-dimensioned mattress with 6-inch-high sides and quilting that would do the best-made bed proud. Rolling off it is impossible, and sleeping on it is like sleeping on a cloud. It's called a Ponderosa Quilted Mattress and costs $6.95.

Two other gadgets belong in this department too. One is an air pump. For some strange reason, mattress manufacturers see fit to provide an aperture for inflation no bigger than the valve of an inner tube. It must be because they want to sell air pumps, because that's what it takes to inflate an air mattress unless you've got a lot of wind or like to get dizzy.

Air pumps sell for around $6, and they come in hand-operated or foot-operated styles. The foot type is the easiest.

If you don't want to go through the troubles of inflation and deflation, and have extra room in your car trunk, you might also consider a foam sleeping pad. They're just about as comfortable as an air mattress, and can be compressed into a smaller bundle than you might think.

SLEEPING IN THE OUTDOORS isn't quite as comfortable as sleeping at home, no matter what your bag or mattress manufacturer might claim. You can make it come close, though, if you'll follow a few simple rules.

Sleep only on level ground. The slightest grade will make quite a difference in your comfort—and how many times you roll out of bed at night.

Sil and I once took my brother on his first camping trip. We went up to an out-of-the-way campsite in New York's Catskills, and got there a little later than we planned. It was taken.

Rather than search for another spot, we pitched a quick camp a few hundred yards down the road on a gentle, grassy knoll, ate dinner, and crawled into our bags. When we awoke the next morning, Bruce was gone.

Both Sil and I assumed that he'd gotten up at the crack of dawn and was out doing something. So we cooked our breakfast and waited around for him to come back.

He finally showed up at ten o'clock, clawing his way up through the brush that surrounded the knoll with his sleeping bag under his arm. He'd rolled off the hilltop and spent the night and half the morning in a thicket of rosebushes.

If you happen to run into a situation like ours that night, and can't find perfectly flat ground, sleep with your feet pointing downhill. You won't be so prone to roll around, and your circulatory system will be doing a normal job of pumping blood.

Everyone seems to have a different idea on what to wear to bed when camping. Theories run the gamut from heavy clothing to au naturel. We find we're most comfortable in a sleeping bag if we sleep in pajamas or loose-fitting clothing (sweatshirts, long johns, and socks) and leave our jeans and outerwear between our bags and air mattress. This keeps them dry of dew, and reasonably warm when we slip them on in the morning.

Maintaining the right temperature inside your bag—not too hot or too cold—isn't as hard as you might think. Since most of us like to camp in warm weather, let's take a look at that end of the scale first.

If your sleeping bag is so warm that it's uncomfortable, open the zipper a bit. This will allow the inside warm air to escape. For quicker cooling you can pull your legs up under you, then stretch them out fast. This has a bellows effect. Warm air is forced out, cool air is sucked in. And you can sleep with the top of the bag tucked under your armpit rather than around your neck. The exposed upper half of your body will radiate heat quickly and keep the rest of you cool.

If cold temperatures and shivering are your problem, here are a few solutions:

• Don't climb into a cold sleeping bag. Warm the inside by the heat of a campfire, tent stove, or car heater.

• Wear plenty of clothes to bed, including a cap, socks, and gloves. Your extremities will be the first to cool off, so if you keep them warm, you'll be warm too.

• Sleep with something between you and the ground. The bottom side of your bag will be compressed tight by your weight and this allows for lots of cold transfer from the ground. Use an air mattress or foam pad. Even a simple canvas or plastic tarp will help a bit.

• If you get cold during the night, slide your head under the covers. The heat of your breath will help warm the inside of your bag, and no body heat will be lost through direct contact with the air.

• If your feet get cold, wrap them up with a jacket or wool shirt.

If you sleep with a pillow at home, sleep with one in the outdoors. We're creatures of habit, and the lack of head support when we're used to it amounts to a pretty radical change. I'm not at all impressed with inflatable pillows either. They make your head sweat, and take off on their own ten times a night. Use a regular pillow, with a pillowcase. If space is a problem, stuff a pillowcase with your clothes. A pillowcase with a zipper can double as a duffel bag too.

104

Everyone has his favorite sleeping position—side, back, stomach. If you can't find your favorite position in a sleeping bag, settle for sleeping on your back with your arms folded across your chest, and learn to live with it. It's the most efficient and effective position when you're inside a close-fitting bag.

QUICK CAMPS AND HOW TO PITCH THEM

Compactness and multipurpose are the key words when you want to pitch a workable camp in a minimum amount of time.

When you're living at a permanent campsite, you have a chance to spread out a bit—to set up areas around the site that can be designated as the larder, the eating area, the living room, and so on. In a quickie camp, your equipment has to be broken out and ready to use in a few minutes' time, and packed up just as fast. You have to take advantage of gear that does more than one job: cooking utensils that double as dishpans, stoves that also function as suitcases.

The essential parts of a camper's day can be divided into three categories: cooking, sleeping, and eating. Let's take a look at each and see how they can be streamlined for maximum performance and comfort with a minimum of effort.

COOKING over a fireplace is out. You probably won't have the time to build a safe fireplace, gather wood, and establish a good bed of coals.

Instead of a fire, rely on a small, two-burner portable stove to warm your meals. These stoves come close to

105

kitchen-range cookery, so there isn't much guesswork involved with dinner and how to get it done. The two most popular kinds of portable stoves use either white gas or bottled gas (liquefied petroleum gas) for fuel. Although there are other kinds of stoves that work quite well, these two are more reliable if for no other reason than that parts and fuel are easy to come by. They also have storage advantages: some of them come with fold-away legs and pack flat; others are housed in boxlike carrying cases permitting you to pack quite a few foodstuffs in with them. Of these small stoves, Thermos, Coleman, Primus-Seivert, and Paulin Infra-Red are products we've tried and liked. (More about stoves, including the question of propane versus white gas cooking, in the following chapter.)

Here are some other ideas related to quickie-camp meals:

• Electric stoves that will cook a full meal have yet to be adapted to camping, but a kind of "mini-stove" is now on the market. It's a drink heater that plugs into your car's cigarette lighter. Just drop the heat coils in any liquid and it soon will be steaming hot. It's perfect for warming children's milk, a quick cup of soup, or your morning coffee.

• When using a standard cookstove, you'll enjoy putting a meal together a lot more if you can work up off the ground. One easy way to make a work surface is to lay some boards across the arms of a chair. Three-foot lengths of 1-by-12-inch board are fine for this, and easy to pack in your car.

• When you're quickie camping, nesting mess kits are a must. Included in one packed-together, bucket-sized unit are cups and plates for four, three cook pots, two skillets, and a coffeepot. If you're cooking for more than four, buy tin plates and you'll be able to fit them in the package too. The container itself is a good-sized bucket that can be used either for cooking or washing up afterwards.

• A few of the modern mess kits boast of Teflon II coating on their skillets and pots. This is a welcome feature as they clean up easily, and don't require great amounts of hard-to-digest grease for proper frying. It's also a wise move to buy the brands that are made slightly squarish. They pack more efficiently in your car, and are more stable around camp.

• Coolers should be included in your camp gear. Since they'll get a lot of handling and knocking around, camp coolers should have a stout metal frame as opposed to the pure styrofoam of the cheaper ones.

A particularly good model for the camper on the move is Coleman's "low boy." It's a high-capacity cooler that takes up surprisingly little room in your car trunk.

Since you'll be on the road quite a bit, and most likely passing through towns, you might not want to carry large stocks of foods that require icing down. If that's your persuasion, don't overlook the insulated plastic "ice satchels." They're soft, waterproof, and will compress to fit in just about any spot. They're perfect for holding sandwich fixings and a six-pack of beer for your noon stop.

When you start off on your trip, you can stock your own ice and save a few cents if you'll freeze up a few water-filled milk cartons. Quart cartons are fine for small coolers, half-gallon or gallon cartons for the large chests. Once that ice melts, you might consider switching to dry ice (if you know where you can find some). It lasts longer than regular ice, keeps things much colder, and evaporates rather than turning to water. Make sure dry ice is protected from direct contact with hands though—it can leave a nasty burn.

THE CAMPANION. Utensils such as knives and forks, can openers, spices, and dry foods are a bit of a problem. Because of their odd shapes and sizes, they don't pack well. Because they're small and there are so many of them, they get packed here and there and keeping track of them is impossible.

This was Sil's biggest problem on our tenting and cross-country camp outs, so she took it in hand and did something about it.

Suitcase for Food Storage

Her solution was what we call the Campanion. It started with an old metal suitcase and a pile of assorted foods and equipment that often turned up on the missing list. Sil bought some elastic banding—the kind you find in the sewing department of any dimestore—and with a "blind

108

riveter" she fastened loops of the elastic to the top half of the suitcase. The loops were made to fit the box of mustard, the salt shaker, the can opener, the spatula, and so on. With the items in place in their loops, she outlined each in pen, then removed it and wrote down what was inside the outline. She did the same with the bottom half of the suitcase, including heavy, bulky foodstuffs and condiments in this deeper section. The result was a carry-anywhere kitchen cabinet that could be set up in seconds.

You don't have to be very handy with tools to make a Campanion, and we both heartily recommend that you take the time. When you do, here are a few points to remember:

• Line the inside of the suitcase with some kind of washable material. Occasionally jelly jars or maple syrup will leak, and this makes cleanup a lot easier.

• When fastening the elastic banding, use a small washer in conjunction with the rivet to keep it from ever pulling through the material.

• Use soft plastic containers for such things as flour, noodles, breakfast cereal, or rice, and write the contents and any instructions on cooking the contents on the top with a marking pen. The plastic is tough enough to resist crushing, tight enough to keep out moisture, and won't break like glass.

• When you use your Campanion, you can set it flat like a chest or hang it from a nail in a tree like a cabinet.

LIGHTS are almost indispensable to comfort. For quickie camping, lights that plug into your cigarette lighter are convenient, and available at most auto supply stores. They come with a 24-foot extension cord. They also make excellent trouble lights should your car quit you after dark. Propane lights are, of course, an alternative.

WATER for cooking, washing, and drinking should be a part of your camp kit. The chances are good that many of your instant campsites won't come with running water, so you'll have to provide it yourself. The best buckets we've found are of collapsible plastic with a turnspout on their top end. They come in a variety of sizes from 1 to 5 gallons and cost from $1 to $3. Be careful where you put them down though—they puncture pretty easily.

EATING. Try to locate your camp near a table, or something that will function as a table. This could be the tailgate of a station wagon, a tree stump, or the top of your cooler.

Use paper plates—not alone, but on top of your mess kit plates. You'll be able to cut your meat without going through to your lap, and won't have a lot of washing to do when you're done.

CLEAN-UP is easiest if you first wipe all your utensils clean with a paper towel or napkin. This gets rid of most of the grease, which is the toughest stuff to cut when you're washing.

If you put a bucket of water on the stove just before you eat, you'll have warm water for the dishes by the time you're done. You may find, as we have, that the easiest method is to wash the dishes with a soap pad and use the wash water as a first rinse.

SLEEPING. Pumping up an air mattress every evening falls

110

a little short of campside fun. If you have the room, leave your air mattress inflated. Since you should never pump them up hard anyway, they'll shape themselves to the contours of a car trunk with only a little persuasion. If you're under a tarp or in a floorless tent, make sure the ground underneath your mattress is swept clean of anything that could puncture it before you lie down.

PITCHING AND STRIKING CAMP work most smoothly if everyone has an assigned task and every item its proper place in your vehicle.

We usually split the chores this way: Sil does the cooking while I pitch the tent, blow up the air mattresses, and unroll the sleeping bags. By then it's time to eat.

We share the cleanup chores.

The next morning, Sil cooks breakfast while I put the sleeping gear back in the car. She packs and checks her kitchen while I wash. Everything goes back into the place from which it came: can opener in the right pocket of the Campanion, unused canned goods into the stove, and all our gear in its appointed place in the car trunk. This is the only way you can keep track of what you've got and what you've used when you're in a hurry.

FOOD FOR THE QUICKIE MEAL

The countless instant and easy-to-prepare meals that line the supermarket shelves today lend themselves particularly well to easy camping. Few of them need refrigeration, most of them are light and compact, and all of them taste a lot better than the questionable powdered eggs and lumpy instant mashed potatoes of twenty years ago.

CAMPING IN COMFORT

All these lightweight foods have one thing in common: their water content has been either severely reduced, or completely removed. In many cases, this is done after cooking, so all you need to do is add water and serve. Breakfast offers a choice that includes:

• Instant oatmeal, flavored with apple or cinnamon and cooked by adding hot water to the bowl you eat from
• Orange juice
• Scrambled egg mix that tastes fresh
• Pancake batter ready to go on the griddle
• Coffee and tea
• Milk with the fat content and good taste of fresh

At breakfast, you might also want to consider the snack packs of dry cereal, packaged in individual serving boxes that double as a bowl.

Dried fruits and raisins will round out your meal. They can be eaten separately, sprinkled on cereal, or mixed right in with pancakes and oatmeal.

For large meals—a heavy lunch or dinner—you can plan on such treats as:

• Freeze-dried T-bone steak, pork chops, and believe it or not, pizza
• Dehydrated vegetables: onions, beans, carrots, and potatoes almost any style
• Instant ice tea or coffee, presweetened fruit drinks, and even powdered cocktail mixes. (You do, unfortunately, have to add a little something more than water to these.)
• Entire dehydrated meals are also available to the sportsman, all placed in one package. Five Star Foods is one manufacturer who offers packaged meals for four in fifteen

separate menus that cover breakfast, lunch, and supper. Most of these dehydrated foods can be bought in stores that cater to back-packers, mountaineers, and skiers.

If you get weary of adding water, you can, of course, supplement your menus with more prosaic foods that fix fast: corned beef hash, stew, canned vegetables, and the old standby of quick cooking, TV dinners.

5 Tent Camping

Many would-be campers have the notion that tenting—except for the purpose of back-pack hiking and quickie camping—is on the way out. They assume that all those bright, shiny pickups and trailer campers, motor homes and live-in vans are gradually replacing canvas around the campsite.

Nothing could be further from the truth. Tents are here today and they're here to stay, and with good reason.

Tents are easily the cheapest camping shelter there is. Prices on a good, serviceable family tent start at around $80, making them a favorite with young families living on a slim budget.

Tents are economical in another way too—they'll still be shedding rain when all of this year's crop of motorized vehicles are nothing but a rusty pile of nuts and bolts. With care, you can plan on a good tent lasting you twenty to thirty years.

And most important, at least to our way of thinking, tents offer the camper mobility, and a chance to live in real wilderness.

When you're on the road, you can pitch your tent anywhere a trailer will go. But if you want to get away from it
all, you can go places with your canvas home where most
wheels fear to tread—a lonely stretch of ocean beach, by
the side of a wild river, or perhaps just a hundred yards or
so back into the trees where you can enjoy privacy and
quiet, away from the grind of traffic.

While we love the comforts of more sophisticated camping gear, both of us agree that if we had but one choice of
outdoor shelters, it would be a tent.

THE TENT FOR YOU—WHAT TO LOOK FOR

If you've got memories of camping with your parents ten
or twenty years ago, don't rely on those past experiences to
provide any clues to what living in today's brand of tent
will be like.

The tents of that day were heavy affairs, hard to pitch,
had little usable living space, and literally stank. Today's
tents are light and airy. They can be bought in some of the
wildest colors this side of a psychedelic circus, and, as the
directions say, they're so simple a child can pitch them—
well, maybe a young adult.

When you shop for a tent, your wife should be with you.
Like a kitchen, a tent is largely a woman's domain, and
her daily housecleaning will be a lot more enjoyable if
she's happy with her home.

Aesthetics and individual preferences aside, here are some
more practical things to look for in making your choice.

TENT MATERIAL should be light, bright, closely-woven cloth.
There are a dozen or more appropriate materials for good

115

tents but they all incorporate several features that you should demand if you want maximum comfort and performance.

The weight of the entire unit (poles, pegs, and cloth) should be light. For an 8-by-8-foot tent, I'd say 40 pounds would be tops. For an 8-by-12-foot tent, 55 to 60 pounds. This not only makes them easier to handle and lug about, but when you get light weight with the other features we'll go into, you're sure to have the quality to boot.

Colors should be bright. Perhaps international orange offends your eye. Well, they don't have to be *that* bright. What we mean is light in color. Bright tent walls mean you'll have plenty of light inside, both from the sun during the day and because of reflected lantern light at night. It also means a good deal of the sun's heat will be reflected too, making your tent at least tolerable on even the warmest days.

Tents shouldn't be waterproofed. They should, of course, shed rain, but they shouldn't do it because the cloth is covered with an oil or paraffin-based mixture.

When closely woven cotton (and most tents are made of high-quality cotton fabrics, or cotton mixed with synthetics) gets wet, it swells. Tent cloth—the kind we recommend—swells so much that it keeps water out. When the tent dries, the cotton shrinks, allowing the inside of the structure to "breathe."

If you have a waterproofed tent, this breathing won't take place, and moisture will build up inside the tent from condensation. The first tent we ever owned was just that kind, and in the warmer months, life inside was a perpetual

116

drizzle. In the early morning and late evening when temperatures fluctuate greatly, it became a downpour.

Another trait of tents with waterproofing is that they smell. As long as the coating is effective, the inside of your tent will have an odor that is a cross between creosote and linseed oil, which could hardly be called pleasant or outdoorsy.

One kind of proofing you do want, however, is fireproofing. You will most likely be using your tent close to a campfire, and on more than one occasion, cooking inside. Make sure the tent you buy is fully fireproofed: floors, walls, and even rope. Don't worry about the odor—fireproofing doesn't smell.

TENT CONSTRUCTION should be rugged, particularly at stress points. Look for double-lap sewing (two parallel seams where cloth joins cloth) and reinforced stress points. These points of stress include places like grommet-fitted corners, wall and roof junctures, and anyplace where the tent joins its pole frame.

Tent size and design are of course important, and we'll talk about them a little later. But, first, here are a few other features to look for in any tent that will function as a home away from home.

• A sewn-in floor. While old-time miners and cowpokes might argue a dewcloth on a floorless tent is better, sewn-in floors make a tent virtually bug and breeze free as well as cleanable. Tent floors will, of course, be of a heavier material than the walls or roof; they have to stand up under quite a bit of foot traffic. A particularly welcome innova-

117

tion in floors that has come into practice in the past few years is to continue them a few inches up the wall. This makes for a leak-free floor and eliminates the necessity for digging a ditch around your tent. Ditching isn't only extra work—it kills sod and destroys the rootwork of trees.

• At least three windows. In conjunction with the doorway, three windows (one in each of the sides, one opposite the entrance) provide cross-ventilation that both cools and dries. The doorway and all windows should have cloth screening to keep bugs out, and flaps that can be tied down to keep warmth in and wind out in cool weather.

• Zipper closures. At least your entrance should be able to be zipped up tight. If you happen to buy the kind of tent that can join up with another, they too should zip together rather than tie together.

• A bug barrier. This is a 3-to-6-inch-high strip that runs across the bottom of the entrance and does a good job of keeping the creepy-crawlies out of your sleeping bags and food stash. It's also touted as a "snake barrier." And if that adds to peace of mind, so be it. Personally, we've never seen a snake inside any kind of tent, "snake barriers" or no, and have never heard a firsthand report from anyone who has.

• Exterior framing. This is easily the most pleasant change in tent construction since tents began. In the past, tent support was always inside, and in your way. Now, frames go up on the outside of your tent, and your home hangs from that exterior support. This is also advantageous in that it creates very little wear on your tent cloth. There's no metal-canvas contact and rub except on the heavy canvas tab-hangers. Leaking is all but eliminated too. In the

118

non-waterproofed kind of tent, leaks will result if anything touches the rain-swollen cloth and initiates capillary action. When tent frames were inside, this was very hard to avoid.

The frames themselves should be light (preferably aluminum) and break down into a small package. Breaking into 4-foot lengths is O.K.; 3-foot lengths are better. Steer clear of the tent poles that telescope. While this appears to be a rather handy setup, three or four years of use is bound to bend these poles, and getting them to slip apart will amount to a family tug-of-war.

• Pitch. In a non-waterproofed tent, pitch is quite important. You need a lot of it to make sure rain will run off, not in. Twenty degrees of pitch on your roof would be rock-bottom; 30 degrees would be better. Your walls should pitch at about 80 degrees. While your walls will never leak per se, any less pitch than that will have water dripping in your windows.

• Pegs. These should be metal and stout. Beware of wire pegs; refuse to accept wooden pegs. Sil and her sewing machine have modified our tent so the peg tabs can't slip over the head of a fifty-penny spike. These are huge nails, 12 inches long and ⅜ of an inch thick. Needless to say, we seldom have trouble with hard, rocky ground.

• Purchase. When you've made your choice of tent, get the salesman to help you set it up. You'll avoid the mental labor of figuring out what the directions really mean when they say, "Place pole A in slot 5." You can also check for pitch, and be sure you're getting all the parts you're supposed to. This is a more common problem than most campers think. We once struggled to figure out a little mountain tent we'd bought, and finally discovered why it had us so

119

baffled: it was missing one pole and the entire zipped-in floor!

And while you're at it, you might ask the salesman to touch a match to the tent corner. If the thing is indeed "fireproof," you'll just get a dab of smoke-soil.

TENT TYPES FOR THE COMFORTABLE CAMPER

There are roughly fifteen basic tent designs available in to-day's camping market, plus variations on the theme that bring the total number of types to near thirty.

Many of those designs are wonderfully suited for specialized camping—the baker tent for the wilderness wanderer, for example. Other good designs, like the parabolic tent, have largely disappeared from the market, and still others, while excellent and functional, simply aren't made properly. The magnificent tipi is a good example of that—even the Indians have largely forgotten how to make this shelter. (If tipis interest you, make sure to read the best book ever written on the subject: *The Indian Tipi* by Reginald and Gladys Laubin, University of Oklahoma Press, 1957.)

Those designs that best suit the average tent camper—the guy who sets up a camp that will be there for two days or more—fall into three categories: the umbrella tent, the extended umbrella, and the cottage tent.

THE UMBRELLA TENT isn't really an umbrella any more. At one time, it was put up by plugging spring-loaded supporting rods into corner holes, then pushing them into place much as one opens an umbrella. But that operation required internal supports.

120

Umbrella tents still have their original shape—four sharply sloping sides and a hip roof that looks like a low, four-sided pyramid—but they're now supported by exterior framing.

Umbrella tents are characteristically square in dimension. The most common sizes are 8 by 8 feet and 10 by 10 feet. This particular design is ideally matched to the camper who does a lot of traveling—not quite enough to qualify him as a "quickie camper," but with a schedule and travel tastes that find him making and breaking camp often.

Umbrella tents go up and come down in less than ten minutes, and take just one man to pitch them. They're extremely sturdy in a high wind too. Because of their squarish dimensions and smallish interior, they're not quite the thing for extended camping in one site.

If a more permanent camp is to your liking you'd do well to consider either an extended umbrella or a cottage tent. They're roomier and a bit more pleasing to the eye.

THE EXTENDED UMBRELLA TENT utilizes the basic design of the umbrella and adds extra space by extending a slope-roofed "room" on one or two sides. The room can be supported either by guys and stakes or, better yet, by external framing. Dimensions start around 8 by 10 feet, and go all the way up to 10 by 16 feet. Some models have sectioned rooms for privacy.

It's this particular design that has our personal stamp of approval. We've tried many kinds, but for camping in a permanent site, or with a few extra for company, a 10 by 14 extended umbrella is tops in our book.

THE COTTAGE TENT, logically enough, looks like a cottage.

121

CAMPING IN COMFORT

It has a house-like roof, and perpendicular walls. This design comes in sizes all the way up to behemoth 10 by 18 dimensions. While cottage tents make living under canvas a lot more like home, they aren't very sturdy in a high wind, and take quite a while to set up. Because of their large wall and roof areas, their material must be a bit stouter than that of umbrella tents, so they're heavy too.

TENT SIZE

What size tent would be best for you? Only you can judge, on the basis not only of size of your family but of what you expect of your canvas home. Here are a few observations Sil and I have made after quite a bit of trial-and-error tenting.

• First, imagine how you would actually live in the tent you're considering. Examine it from the inside and decide where each of you will sleep, where the food will be kept, where the table will go if it showers in time for dinner, and just how much space will be required for the whole family to keep their cool and perspective during a 24-hour rain. We estimate that, for tent camping as opposed to the "quickie" kind, 20 square feet of floor for each camper is a sufficient area for him to exercise his territorial imperative.

• Don't buy too big. Maybe you have eight kids or an army of friends? If that's the case, think about two tents instead of one giant. We usually think of a "family" tent as sleeping four. Maybe five in a pinch, but no more. Six or more people living inside what amounts to one canvas room gets more than hectic—it approaches pandemonium.

• Be sure your tent has plenty of stand-up room. Not just

enough to clear your haircut when you stand in one spot, but enough for you to walk around a bit. There should also be space for storage of more gear than you anticipate bringing, because chances are that's just how much you *will* bring.

TENT CARE

Your canvas home will last you a lot longer if you give it a reasonable amount of care.

The first place tents begin to show wear is on the floor. Keep the canvas swept clean and you'll omit abrasive pebbles, sticks, and sand that cause most of the damage. When a hole appears, patch it by either sewing or gluing a piece of canvas over the hole.

When you finally fold up your tent and leave, make sure you clean it and dry it before storage. Since morning and evening air is bound to be damp, if you break camp at those times, remember to stretch your tent over a few lawn chairs at home, or hang it on the line so it can be packed away bone-dry. Stowing canvas when it's wet or damp is the quickest route to rot and ruin.

Your tent should be clean when you put it away too. Scrape any bird droppings or pine resin off the material. General dust and dirt will come clean by a vigorous brushing with a soft broom. If you've torn a hole in your roof or walls during the trip, the best repair to make is with fabric cement and a matching patch on the outside. Sewing leaves little holes in the material that might leak at a later time.

Tent poles need a little attention too. Any kind of metal corrodes, particularly when you're around ocean beaches.

123

CAMPING IN COMFORT

With the new exterior framing, this is even more prevalent.

To make sure you'll be able to pitch camp in a hurry next time, lightly swab any metal poles with oil before you store them for the season. Pay particular attention to male/female joints.

Although we like to carry our tent pegs, poles, and canvas all wrapped up in one unit, it isn't a good idea to pack them for an entire winter that way. The metal (especially steel pegs) might corrode a bit, and stain your light-colored tent material. There's also more than an off-chance that they'll cause a crease in your tent that will later leak.

Because creasing can cause leaking, it's also a good idea to put your tent away loosely rolled. You might also unroll it and reroll it once during the off-season.

TENTING PROBLEMS

No matter how expensive a tent you've bought, it just isn't as sturdy and well built as the home you live in, and you can expect a few problems. But they'll be minor, and so will their solution.

Here's a sampling of a few of the more common ones:

• A leak. This is usually the result of someone brushing the wet canvas and beginning capillary action—not a fault of the tent. You can either put a pan under it, or pin a string at the point of the leak, then lead the end to wherever you want it to drip (this trick is handy if you've got a leak right over your sleeping area). Because there's no pressure of thread on the pinhole, it will close itself up in due time. Of course, it's better not to touch the wet canvas in the first place.

124

If your leak is obviously the result of thin cloth or a minor abrasion in a small spot, you can cure it quickly by rubbing candlewax or paraffin onto the spot. Chapstick will work if nothing else is handy.

If you just bought a new tent and the whole thing seems full of leaks, don't get too excited. The tent has to be shrunk before it will work right. Because of this, the practice of backyard camping to familiarize yourself with new equipment is doubly important. Set your tent up and spray it with a garden hose.

No matter where your new tent is set up, remember to loosen your guys and pegs if it's going to rain. Things are bound to get a little tight because of shrinkage. While this is largely accepted as standard procedure every time it rains, we've found that after about five good showers, tents don't exhibit a very wide range of expansion and contraction. They do exhibit enough, however, to make loosening up a wise practice if you've got your tent stretched tight as a drumhead and anchored to hard-holding soil.

• A hole is a very good reason for a leak, and infinitely easier to comprehend than shrinkage, expansion, and capillary action. You can temporarily patch a hole with wide adhesive tape if you're not prepared to do the permanent patching job (with fabric cement and tent material) right away. Do both from the outside. Of course, if it's raining when you happen to discover your hole, neither method will work since nothing sticks to wet material. Put a dinner plate over the hole, and maybe a pan under it.

• Hard-fitting poles. To cure this problem, buff all joints with light emery cloth. If emery isn't a part of your camp kit, try sand or dirt. Before refitting, wash the joints with

125

water, get them thoroughly dry, and apply a little oil (you can get a drop of oil from the dip stick in your car engine).

• Missing poles. Occasionally you might lose part or all of a pole and be unaware of it until you pitch the next camp. Exterior-framed tents have another advantage—you can pitch them with ropes to tree limbs. Your tent won't be quite so taut and waterproof without its original framing, but it's better than catching a shower all over your sleeping bag.

• Missing pegs. If you've misplaced a peg or two, don't worry too much unless you expect a gale. Peg the tent corners down first, worry about the middle stake tabs last. If you're really in need of some pegging tie-downs, in soft soil you can use a coat-hanger wire, in hard or rocky soil you can tie a length of rope to a small log, then bury it and tie the other end of the rope to your stake tab.

• Soft soil takes tent pegs nicely, but carries a problem all its own: tent poles want to sink down in it. Keep them up where they should be by setting them in wide tin cans or coffee-can lids. Even flat rocks will work if you have no discarded cans.

EQUIPMENT THAT SPELLS COMFORT

You live in a tent, selected with care. You live with and by the equipment you bring; its nature and variety should be selected with even greater care.

What's the difference between a cumbersome gimcrack and a necessity? Space-consuming addenda and a welcome luxury?

It's impossible to establish any hard-and-fast rules, but

here are a few things we've learned about equipment to buy and bring, and the comfort it provides.

• Any equipment that gets your camp closer to home-style comfort is welcome. It's more pleasant to sit on a chair than on a log; sleeping on a mattress is infinitely more pleasurable than on hard ground; eating at a table with a tablecloth makes a meal taste better than eating from your lap.

• Equipment that offers home comfort should be surrogate equipment, specifically designed for camping. It would be absurd to bring your favorite easy chair on a camping trip—or your inner-spring mattress. Bring substitutes that fit into the camping scene: an aluminum deck chair and air mattress. There's a more subtle, but still valid difference between kitchen-cabinet fry pans and nesting mess kits, a pile of blankets and a sleeping bag, and a water tumbler of glass and one of plastic or paper.

• When making your equipment list, do it in order of importance to your comfort. In other words, we make sure we pack a good tent before we pack deck chairs. We find the room for our sleeping bags and air mattresses before we take a cot. We pack a campstove before we decide on whether or not to take a barbecue grill, and include deck chairs before we consider a portable TV.

Personal preferences are, of course, going to make a difference too. If you're an avid fisherman, a rod and reel will be one of the first things to be included. The length of your stay is another determining factor. It's a little silly, and a lot of work, to pitch a big camp complete with a dining fly and barbecue grill if you're only going to be there overnight.

CAMPING IN COMFORT

But assuming that, like us, you enjoy camping for an extended period of time and really appreciate comfort and convenience, here's a rundown on the complementary equipment we like to bring, and why.

CAMPSTOVES are the single biggest worksaver you'll ever find around camp. Compare building a fire, getting a good bed of coals, then cooking three meals a day over uneven heat, to the turn of a dial. You'll come up with about two hours' time and a lot of labor saved.

We're not recommending you use only your campstove. An evening meal cooked over an open fire is part and parcel of camping fun. But an awful lot of that fun wafts away like smoke when you have to go through the work of building a fire every time you want to eat something hot. This is especially true of breakfast.

When it comes to types, we prefer three-burner stoves for a semi-permanent camp. Most meals are three-dish affairs, and with these you can get all three done and ready to eat at the same time.

White-gas stoves are the cheapest to buy and operate, but unless you've got a little mechanical savvy, they're often a problem to keep working right. The stove must be perfectly level, it has to be pumped up every once in a while to hold a hot flame, and should you make a mistake and fuel it with either auto gas or white gas from a dirty container, you'll have to go through a major overhaul before it will work again.

Propane stoves are the most convenient and the safest camp ranges. To make them work, all you have to do is hook up the propane and turn a dial, just like a gas range at home. They used to be powered by throwaway gas

128

Commercial campgrounds of today include more than a tent site. Horseback riding, fishing, golfing, and swimming pools are often a part of the package they offer. *(See page 21.)*

The lightness and compactness
of mountain-camping
equipment make it suitable
for quickie camping as well as
wilderness wandering.
(See pages 96 to 98.)

Quickie camping is a good solution to the crowded campground problem. Any wooded lane amounts to a perfect site. *(See pages 96 and 97.)*

Modern tents are bright, airy, and—thanks to exterior framing—roomy and long-lasting. *(See pages 121 and 122.)*

A good example of what compact comforts can be had by the modern camper is this stove/light combination by Paulin Infra-Red Products. Other appliances (refrigerators and heaters) can be attached to the propane umbilical cord, and the top of the stove doubles as a dishpan. *(See pages 128 and 129.)*

A carrying case is a welcome adjunct to any camp lighting system. In addition to break-free storage of your lamp, the case holds extra fuel and mantles. *(See pages 130 and 131.)*

Propane catalytic heaters warm you with the turn of a dial and touch of a match. Their heat can also be directed. *(See pages 132 and 133.)*

BernzOmatic's jet fogger keeps insects away from camp for up to ten hours. It's powered by propane. *(See page 137.)*

Camper trailers are popular because of their roominess when set up, and compactness under tow. *(See pages 140 to 142.)*

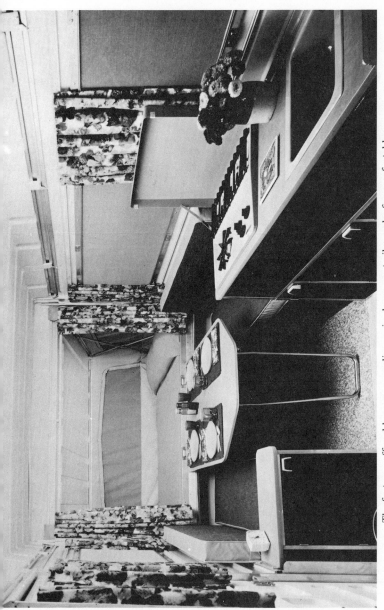

The features offered by even a medium-priced camper trailer make for comfortable, efficient living. (See page 141.)

Airstream Trailer's unique "monocoque" construction and thoughtful design mean easy trailering and easy outdoor living. *(See page 146.)*

This rugged four-wheel drive Jeep is specially designed to carry a camper home. It is one of the most mobile for back-country travel. *(See page 148.)*

Large motor homes offer the ultimate in comforts, including the fact that the driver is always "home." (See pages 150 and 151.)

Spacious and extensive appointments make large motor homes the first choice for extended living "on the road." (*See pages 150 and 151.*)

Camping with a car topper means that you can pitch your camp anywhere the water touches shore. *(See page 165.)*

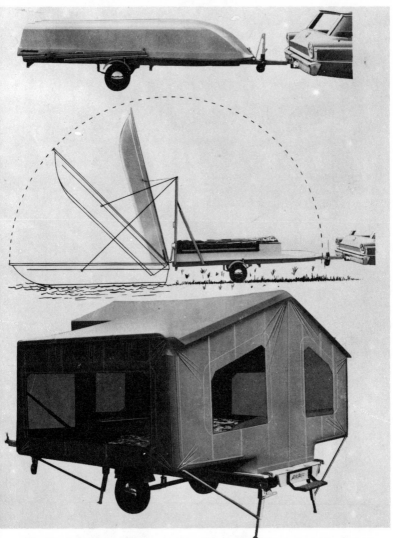

The Mossberg Marine Camper combines fun on the water and a tent shelter for four—all in the same package. *(See page 177.)*

Camp-R-Cruise offers this mini-houseboat, functional on both land and sea. It can

Lots of living space crammed into a small car plus low gas mileage make the VW "Campmobile" a popular vehicle for European campers. Best news for Americans, it can be bought more cheaply overseas than back home. (See page 207.)

This sharp-looking prototype sportster amounts to the dune buggy of the future. Built by Jeep Corporation, it boasts four-wheel drive, extra-wide tires, and a reinforced plastic body. *(See pages 227 to 229.)*

Light weight and a large payload make small canoes ideal craft for anglers and hunters, or campers bent on exploring. *(See page 233.)*

All Terrain Vehicles do just about everything—swim, crawl through mud and snow, and whiz across sand. *(See page 233.)*

bottles that were both expensive and inefficient, but now you can use a refillable reservoir bottle. This increases their performance, capacity, and efficiency, and somewhat lowers fuel costs. It also allows you to hook up an octopus of stove, tent heater, lights, and even a portable refrigerator if you wish—all powered by the central fuel cylinder.

Whatever your choice of fuels, the campstove for the tent camper should break down to provide easy access for cleaning up spilled foods and spattered grease. The stove should also incorporate some kind of wind baffle so you can keep the wind away from your flame, and the heat where it belongs—under the food.

The entire unit should fold up into some kind of protective case. Aside from keeping the delicate working parts of a stove away from harm, this also keeps gear that might be packed nearby away from staining grease and soot.

Most brands of campstoves also offer the camper a stand-up cooking platform that folds away when not in use. Buying these along with your stove is a wise move, since they mean you'll be cooking up off the ground.

Coolers come in a wide range of sizes and styles, but our favorite for tent camping is the stand-up kind that opens like an icebox. It has separate compartments for foodstuffs and ice, and its design is such that you don't have to dig through three layers of things to find the lemon that sifted down to the bottom.

These are, of course, the most expensive of the cooler models. If you want to economize and buy the standard chest cooler, here are a few tips on getting better performance from them.

Always pack the heaviest items on the bottom—cans of

beer and soda and other liquids that need refrigeration. Pack meats on top of that, and fragile fresh vegetables (lettuce, tomatoes, corn) on top of the meat. Most chest coolers include a small tray that fits in the top. This is best used when it holds the items you're likely to reach for most: butter, eggs, and any dishes of last night's leftovers (though considering typical camp appetites, there shouldn't be many).

Remember, too, that ice cools most efficiently when it's *above* the objects to be refrigerated. That's because cold air sinks. Conversely, if you for some reason want to conserve ice, pack it low.

Don't forget to utilize the cooling effect of frozen foods. When we go camping far from civilization and a source of ready ice, we stock up heavily on frozen meats and vegetables and plan to eat them the second and third day. This often eliminates the need for space-taking ice entirely, giving us more packing room for foods.

Always refrigerate any foodstuffs previous to packing your cooler. And it doesn't hurt to cool your cooler off with a tray of ice cubes before you fill it.

LIGHTS are a virtual necessity whatever your camping persuasion. Of the kinds available, three are of prime interest to the camper.

• Electric lights have come a long way since the day of the flashlight. Powered by 6-volt lantern batteries, they come in attractive designs and even include neon bulbs. Their advantages are that they don't produce much heat for the light they throw, they're on at the flick of a switch, and they don't require ignition. They are a bit expensive to keep powered however. They last between 3 and 6 hours on two batteries.

• LP gas or propane lights are economical and start to work with the turn of a dial and touch of a match. They throw quite a glow when turned on full. Most of the lights in this class work on throwaway cans of pressurized gas. In the stove/light combination such as the Paulin Infra-Red, the light can be popped free of its gas-tank umbilical cord, and a portable can of bottled gas snapped in its place.

• White-gas powered lights are the most economical of all, but they must be pumped up previous to lighting. Because they incorporate more working parts than either the electric or propane light, they also tend to go on the fritz more often.

When choosing your camp lights, make sure whatever style you buy can break down for easy packing. If it doesn't, you'll end up with a broken globe every time. Both Coleman and Smith-Victor Corporation offer a "light kit" for the camper. Space for fuel, extra mantles, funnels, and the light itself is provided in one cushioned carrying case.

The best arrangement we've found for camp illumination is two lights. One, a double-mantle white-gas powered lamp, can be used to light up the outdoors area. A light that does a job like that tends to be turned on and off once an evening, so pumping shouldn't get to be a chore.

The second light, either gas or electric, can be used inside your tent. It'll be on in a second should you be roused out of the sack at four in the morning.

COTS. Generally, cots aren't really needed for comfort. There's no more comfortable bed than an air mattress on

131

flat ground. However, humans are creatures of habit, and often people sleep better if they're off the ground and in a bed like the one they left at home. If this is your persuasion, then bring a cot by all means. Steer clear of the folding contraptions that come in small packages. They don't last very long. The best kind to get is the simplest—aluminum-framed cots with legs that fold flat, and a hinge in the middle.

This kind of cot also comes in a model that permits you to nest one on top of the other to make bunk beds. They're always a favorite with the kids and amount to a real spacesaver in a tent.

Talking about spacesavers, we always bring at least one cot with us for that very reason. Set up in the tent, it frees floor space underneath for storage, and equipment kept there isn't disturbed when you make your bed.

HEATERS are a real blessing if you're camping in cool climates or at chilly times of the year. They not only provide warm inside temperatures, they also keep the dampness burned out.

There are two kinds of heaters well suited to tent camping: gasoline heaters and radiant propane heaters. They both use a catalytic process rather than an open flame to generate heat, reducing deadly carbon monoxide emission to an acceptable minimum. But again, don't forget that although catalytic heaters produce virtually no carbon monoxide, they do use up oxygen as they burn and should not be used in tightly sealed structures such as small travel trailers or station wagons without letting in some air.

Gasoline heaters take about a half hour to achieve full

132

output, but they're the most inexpensive of the two to operate. They do, however, require white gas, which is sometimes hard to find. If you use them with regular leaded gasoline, you'll get incomplete combustion, resulting in carbon monoxide.

Radiant propane heaters are on and working at the turn of a dial and touch of a match. Their heat can also be directed—concentrated toward your dining area, sleeping area, or a line of wet clothes. They can be fueled either by a small, portable bottle of gas or one of the large refillable containers, used in conjunction with other LP appliances.

Heaters are rated by BTU's (British Thermal Units). A 5,000-BTU heater will keep a 10-by-12 tent close to 70 degrees when the temperature is in the thirties outside. A gasoline heater will last around 16 hours on a filling of fuel. Propane is, of course, determined by the capacity of the cylinder you're using.

CHAIRS are truly welcome and often overlooked by the beginning camper. There's a world of relaxing difference between squatting on the ground and sitting up off it with some support for your back. The most practical chairs we've come across are the lawn variety (with arms) in lieu of the more standard "card chairs."

Buy them in aluminum for lightness, and don't get the most expensive models either. Quality lawn chairs are usually of good-sized dimensions, and take up quite a bit of room when they're packed. The smaller, cheaper chairs still provide lots of sitting room and support, but are more economical in terms of space and of cash spent.

TABLES should be included if you know the area you're

133

going to doesn't have any. Here, the flat-folding "card table" works very well. Chairs and tables are also a smart item to include in your gear list when you're trailer camping. They allow you freedom to enjoy living outside your walls.

Another item that goes hand in hand with chairs and tables is the . . .

DINING FLY. This piece of equipment amounts to little more than a square tarp, pitched with aluminum poles to make a roof. There are no walls to a dining fly. It makes for a place outside the confines of a tent where you can escape the noonday sun or a sudden shower. Cooking, too, is more pleasant under the protection of a fly. It's also a great place for the kids to play while you "escape" from them.

You can build a makeshift fly out of a canvas or plastic tarp, using the principles explained in "Quickie Camping." To our way of thinking, though, you're ahead of the game if you buy one factory made, complete with poles, guys, and canvas.

BARBECUE GRILLS, assuming you like to barbecue and can afford the space, are a great help too. They offer stand-up cooking, and are a little bit more dependable in terms of results than a pit dug into the ground.

Don't buy a big monstrosity on wheels; just a simple pan and grill with folding legs works fine and doesn't take up much packing room. A wind baffle is about the only other accoutrement you might consider—but only if it will fold up flat for storage.

When starting your charcoal, here's a tip that will save a lot of waiting. Pile your charcoal *on top* of the grill and get it started there. Either build a fire under it in the pan or use charcoal starter. Getting things going this way allows plenty of air to get to the coals and gets them glowing fast. Once they're covered with white ash and ready for cooking, dump them off the grill and into the pan underneath. Of course, use gloves or potholders for this operation.

WHAT'S NEW UNDER THE SUN?

A love of gadgetry and new inventions is as American as apple pie. Each year sees a hundred or so "new" products hit the camping and outdoor market, and many of them disappear soon after their introduction. Here's a sampling of a few products that seem to have clicked, and proven their usefulness in terms of comfort and modern convenience around the camp.

SHELTER. The concept of tents and what they should be is suddenly changing. Rather than making tents larger and larger, many manufacturers are making a small, basic tent that will zip up to another like it. You can increase or decrease the size and capacity of your canvas home by adding or removing each separate unit.

These tents can also be pitched singly, and several styles are being produced that will snug right up to an auto camper body, offering more room for storage when you're living on wheels.

REFRIGERATION

• A car-cooler—a true refrigerator that runs off your car battery. It also will work off an LP gas supply, and can even be plugged into your 110-volt socket at home!

• Small coolers for specialized use. One model is just the

right size for a six-pack of beer or pop, and the ice to cool it. It's perfect if small boating is part of your camping trip. Another kind of cooler amounts to an insulated jug that keeps ice separate from the contents by enclosing it in a waterproof plastic container. It's a great mini-icebox for small items, and a perfect companion for the serious social drinker who doesn't like watered-down martinis.

LIGHTING is made easy by a three-way electric light. It can be powered from its own portable batteries, plugged into your car's electrical system, or used in a standard 110-volt outlet.

COOKING around camp is getting as easy as in any kitchen.
 • Dupont's Teflon II has already been mentioned in connection with quickie camping; needless to say, it's handy to have for camping any style. This coating makes cleanup a breeze. And it's tough enough so you don't have to use special utensils.
 • White-gas cooking stoves can be converted to propane or LP gas with a special conversion kit if you get tired of pumping.
 • A complete camp kitchen is available as a kit or finished product. Utensils aren't provided, but a place to keep them is. (This unit is a lot bigger than our Campanion and not suited to quickie camping.)
 • When cooking's over and it's time to do the dishes, Gloy's, Inc., sells a folding dishpan that holds 2 gallons of water. This rubberized canvas bowl doubles as a baby bassinet or bathtub.

SITTING
 • Plastic blow-up chairs. They're a little sticky on hot nights, and don't get them too near sparks or sit them on

136

sharp rocks, but all in all, their compactness when deflated, and comfort when inflated, make them a natural for reading or relaxing over cocktails at the end of the day. You'd also better be long winded if you're going to blow them up by mouth or get an . . .

• Electric air pump that plugs into your auto's cigarette lighter. These are also great if you're carrying some sort of inflatable boat, and work equally well on an air mattress.

While you're sitting around, there's a good chance insects might join you for the evening. If you don't like their company, you can give them the bum's rush with a portable . . .

• Insect fogger. A gadget that works on propane and sends out a cloud of mist that works as a bug-killer for hours. This isn't just a good hand around camp, it's good for patio parties, barbecues, and picnics.

CLEANING

• Fold-away showers, complete with a canvas bucket and spray nozzle over your head, are handy when the water's too cold or polluted for swimming. If it's your living quarters you want to clean up, consider . . .

• A collapsible broom. The short handle makes for easy storage, and without the handle the head can be used as a whisk broom.

SLEEPING

• Paper sleeping bags are warm enough for summer camping and can be thrown away or burned when you're done with them.

• Paper blankets generate their own heat. They can be

used in conjunction with a light sleeping bag to make it warmer, or with a bedroll.

• Paper sheets and pillowcases eliminate a lot of laundry when you get back from your trip. Use the sheets for sleeping bag liners. All paper sleeping gear feels a bit like flannel to the touch and doesn't crinkle, crackle, or crunch when you roll over.

• Triple-temperature sleeping bags amount to three sleeping bags in one. They fit one inside the other. On warm nights, one will keep you cool. On cool nights, two will keep you comfortable. On downright cold nights, use three and you'll be warm.

ELECTRIC GENERATORS that run on regular gas aren't as big as a bread box, and don't make any more noise than a decidedly muffled put-put. They have enough output to run several electric lights or one juice-pulling appliance, like a toaster, electric fry pan, or radiant heater.

Another electrifying addition to the camper's grab bag is a portable, rechargeable battery pack. It's made by Centralab and costs in the neighborhood of $60. It won't turn out 110 volts as do gasoline generators, but it has enough power to handle most battery-operated devices. Electric typewriters are now made to work off these powerpacks and so are . . .

PORTABLE TV's. They're small and compact, with black and white models weighing less than 15 pounds. Color units weigh less than 30 pounds. Most models can be run off both batteries and regular house outlets.

PORTABLE TOILETS are the ultimate in camping in style. The best models flush just like the real thing, and can be used up to thirty times before they need recycling.

6 Recreational Vehicle Camping

I'll never forget the first "recreational vehicle" I ever saw. It was a crude, windowless wooden affair, perched on the back of a pickup owned by a devoted surf-caster.

"Hank," I asked him, "what the devil are you going to do with that thing?"

"It's perfect for me," he replied. "With 'that thing' on the back, all I've got to do is find out where the fish are, then catch them. I can drive right up and get to work. If they move, so can I. And without taking the time to break up camp and pack."

"Well," I grumbled, "maybe it's a good thing for surf-casting, but I don't quite see how it will ever replace a tent."

I see now. As a matter of fact, the patent rights on the basic camper design are second only to those on the wheel in my estimation of what would constitute a good investment.

Campers, camper trailers, travel trailers, and motor homes are all categorized as "recreational vehicles," "rec-

139

vees" for short. They're a home on wheels for the traveling man and boast of nearly every convenience you'd expect to find behind your front door. They've experienced a phenomenal growth in popularity in the past ten years, and with excellent reason.

They virtually eliminate motel bills, the cost of eating in restaurants, and the "work" of camping with canvas. They're so popular with the touring vacationer that they blossom like wild roses on summer highways from coast to coast.

They're snug, comfortable shelters in cold weather too. Consequently, they rate high with fishermen, hunters, skiers, and snowmobilers. More than any other outdoor innovation, they've made winter a camping "season" like any other.

CAMPER TRAILERS

Camper trailers were once commonly called tent trailers, but that term is on the way out. The reason is that very few of them nowadays have an exclusively canvas roof.

A camper trailer is a low, boxy trailer that packs a pop-up home inside its frame. They range in size from tiny 7-by-4-foot-models, all the way up to 7-by-14-foot homes. The small models operate by muscle, the large ones by electric crank, but both flop out, frame up, and blossom into sizable shelters on wheels.

There are two basic categories of camper trailers: soft tops and hard tops. Soft tops are the true tent trailers. On these units, the top of the trailer itself is split and folds

140

out from the middle to make beds. Rods are anchored to these outer extremities and up goes the canvas, supported by a folding, hinged frame. These camper trailers are the lightest recvees to tow, will cover the roughest country, and they're the most inexpensive at prices that start around $300. They also have the fewest appointments—usually just two beds, a walkway, a roof over your head, and sometimes a dinette area.

The hard-top camper trailers have a solid one-piece cover over the box. The top goes straight up, and when in place, extensions fold out from either end. On the most expensive models, the walls are telescoping fiberglass or ABS plastic; on others, they're just canvas.

These units start around $1,000 and go up to $3,000. They also boast of some homey appointments: permanent stoves, refrigerators, toilets, heating plants, and sleeping accommodations for between six and eight adults. One plush model we know of has all the cooking appliances aligned on a sliding roller door that can be opened from the outside. This means you don't have to pitch the whole home if you want to make a noon lunch stop.

The advantages of a camper trailer over permanently placed walls on wheels all start in the pocketbook. In terms of the number of people that they can handle for the cash spent, they're way out ahead of whatever is in second place. As a result, they're most popular with young recvee-ers, who have a limited budget but like to travel.

Saving in initial cost isn't the only way they're easy on the pocketbook though. Because they're light in weight and low in profile, they're easy to trailer. Wind doesn't bother them and they won't lug on hills. That means a savings in gas. Their low, light construction means a few other things too—you won't need any weight-equalizer hitches, or giant stick-out mirrors to see who's behind you.

Camper trailers are popular with sportsmen as well as young families. They're easy to snake into and out of rough country, and should you hit a dead-end road, the weight on their tongue is light enough so they can be unhitched and turned around by hand. When they're not in use, that lightness means they can be jockeyed into a corner of your yard, the back of your garage, or even block-and-tackled into the rafters of a storage shed.

All isn't roses with camper trailers though. Like everything else in the world, they have their good points and their bad.

At least to our way of thinking, two of their biggest disadvantages are that they're chilly in cool weather, virtually eliminating them from contention as a winter camper; then there's the perpetual trailer problem—you can't tote a trailered boat.

Of course, perhaps you like neither water sports nor winter. If that's the case, there are just a few more little things you might find bothersome. Consider them before you buy.

Some camper trailers—especially the big ones—have been known to twist and torque themselves out of kilter after a few years' worth of chuckholes. As a result, the precision mechanism used to raise and lower the structure doesn't line up properly, and they get jammed up or down.

We're not saying all big camper trailers have this problem, just enough to make it worth mentioning. But still, you might talk with somebody who's been a two-or-more-year owner of the brand you're thinking of buying.

Access is another minor problem. In most models, you have to pitch the whole house to get inside for a sandwich or a fishing rod. And because the thing collapses, you have to store those fishing rods, your clothes, and anything taller than 2 feet, flat on the floor.

When you buy a camper trailer—any recvee for that matter—you're wise to stick with a name brand—a name you recognize and see a lot of around the campgrounds. Service and dealer interest in your problems are one consideration. Then, too, chances are that brand wouldn't be so popular if it had some inherent failings.

A few other things to look for in any camper trailer you plan to call home include:

• Ease of operation. Ask the salesman to explain how to make the thing go up. If it's a rather simple operation—simple to master with only a few steps to follow—you're pretty sure of a well-designed lowering and raising mechanism. According to Fineagle: "The chances for a mechanical breakdown are directly proportional to that object's number of moving parts."

• Along those same lines, inspect the bed of the trailer for close-fitting joints, and the closed trailer for a tight-fitting top. A good seal all the way around means no road dust will get inside to clog mechanisms and dirty the interior.

• Make sure your trailer comes with an extra wheel. It's

143

a sure bet that the tire from your car won't fit your camper trailer, and those small, odd-sized tires aren't easy to come by in small towns.

TRAVEL TRAILERS

Travel trailers have permanent walls. Their dimensions run all the way from compact 10-footers to 30 feet and longer.

Although it's something of an arbitrary rule of thumb, most trailers over 32 feet are classified as mobile homes. These large living quarters are designed for a minimum amount of trailering and a lot of sitting in one spot. They're too big to hold up under the strain of bumpy roads and frequent moves.

Even 32 feet is quite a load for the average car to lug around, and consequently, the most popular length for travel trailers falls somewhere around 22 feet.

In terms of living in travel trailers, foot-for-foot they come the closest to home. The interior has a generally uncrowded look about it, and in fact is. They're easy to move around in, cook in, and live in. You don't feel cramped, and the appointments are usually more extensive and better-placed than an equivalently priced truck camper or medium-sized motor home.

Most travel trailers in the 22-foot category incorporate a complete kitchen, sleeping for up to six, a toilet, and shower. Larger units can be bought with many options: a stereo tape deck, an electric generator all their own, air conditioning, and even a full-sized bathtub. Generally, trailers up to 20 feet in length have two wheels. Those larger than that have four. Prices on travel trailers start at $800 for a stripped-down job, and can go as high as $10,000 for the luxury models.

The advantages of a travel trailer include several of those features found in a camper trailer: in both, once you set up "camp," you can leave your home where it is and roam around in the car. You don't have to pack away dishes and grub every time you want to go shopping or see the sights. Another similarity between the two becoming evident in newer models is fold-out rooms. Several trailer manufacturers offer models that have extra living space that accordions into the trailer body when you're underway. Travel trailers are also the most popular form of recvees, constituting about 40 per cent of the market, and as a result, they hold a high resale value.

Although one of the most endearing features of any trailer is that you can use the family buggy to haul them around, you'll need some special equipment to get the job done.

If your tongue weight (the pressure the trailer exerts on your car hitch) exceeds 150 pounds, you'll have to have a special load-leveling hitch installed. These hitches have to be balanced with your trailer and are welded right to your car frame.

Most trailers incorporate electric brakes of their own, so you'll have to get the hookup unit installed too. And special mirrors so you can see around your wide, high load.

Two other problems should be considered by the prospective trailer owner. The most common is where to store

145

them. Many towns have zoning ordinances that prohibit any kind of trailer homes within a certain district. You can't even park them on your own property. One solution is to park them in your garage—if they'll fit—and leave your car outside. Another is to rent some storage space nearby.

The second problem is prohibition on certain roads. Large cities often limit their freeways and main traffic arteries to cars only. This eliminates trucks and any kind of trailer, whether it be used for recreational purposes or not. Before you settle on a trailer as your camp on wheels, it might pay to find out if you'll have to buck city traffic and stop lights every time you want to head for the hills.

If you decide that a travel trailer suits your outdoor tastes, here are a few things to consider before you buy.

Make sure the floor has a good, solid feel to it. This is an indication of solid framing underneath. You'll be a lot happier with your unit and its road performance if most of the weight that it carries is low and close to the floorline. This means easy and stable trailering. A contoured jet-stream design (called monocoque design) is another plus factor. It's borrowed from airplane construction, and means great strength with little weight. A streamlined design also cuts down on air drag, side-wind effect, and, as a result, your gasoline bill while you're underway.

Joints between the roof, walls, and floor should be close-fitting, and rivets should be placed so as to create tight seams. Avoid any product that's put together with nails or common screws; it's bound to fall apart after those nails work loose from road vibration. Tongue weight is

146

another sign of quality. Even the largest travel trailers shouldn't exert more than 500 pounds of hitch pressure.

Unless you're buying both car and trailer, the weight of your family buggy will play a part in your trailer selection. Under no circumstances should your trailer be heavier than your car.

You might also make a careful self-examination of what you want to use your travel trailer for. If you're an avid outdoorsman, keep the conveniences on the spare side, and the weight and length of the unit to a minimum. Travel trailers are notoriously limiting when you want to take them along on a back-country expedition.

TRUCK CAMPERS

Truck campers are a vehicle and portable home that share the same wheels. The living quarters are a separate unit that either slides into the bed of a pickup truck or is bolted directly to the truck chassis. Truck campers range in appointments from the bare walls and interior of a "truck cap" (also called a camper shell) to the plush built-on-the-frame homes that boast a toilet, a shower, and beds for eight.

In the middle of this broad spectrum, you'll find the most popular units. They're usually of slide-in design, and include cooking and eating facilities, a large double bed that stretches over the cab of the truck, and a dinette that makes into a bed for two. Other bunks often fit in here and there, so you can, in a pinch, sleep up to six. But that many bodies accounts for quite a crowd in even the larg-

147

est camper. In camper homes whose floor space is longer than 8 feet, toilets and showers can be included, and this self-containment feature is becoming a popular trend.

Except in the case of built-on campers, the camper can be removed from the truck with about a half-hour's work. When your camping trip is over, you have a second car for the family. And don't get the idea that a modern pickup truck is a "truck" circa 1950. They ride every bit as smoothly as the family sedan, have roomy interiors, and can be bought with options such as power brakes and steering, automatic transmission, and air conditioning.

The advantages of a truck camper are all derived from the fact that your home rides on the same wheels you do. This means mobility for off-the-road exploring, plus room for a trailer should you want to bring a large boat or extra gear.

If back-country exploring interests you, you might also do well to look into the pop-top campers. They're a little like camper trailers in that they telescope down out of the way, level with the cab when you're on the road, then pop up into full-sized walking room when you're ready to live in them. This means less wind resistance on the open highway and a lower center of gravity when you're in the hills. And don't think that gravity doesn't play a part in truck camper mobility. They're touted for their ability to get into rough country, but some large campers we've driven were so top heavy that we were afraid to take them on a sidehill.

A truck camper's turtle nature offers a few other problems too. The biggest is that your "camp" must be struck every time you want to move. Dishes and bedding must be

148

put away, and everything that might move lashed down.

This isn't much of a problem when you're gypsy camping—resting at night and covering ground during the day. But say you're on a vacation in Yellowstone National Park. You find a pleasant slot for your vehicle, cook lunch, then want to go and see Old Faithful. You've got to pack everything in for the trip, and probably will lose your spot to another camper. The same thing will happen every time you want to see the sights beyond camp.

Because they have a narrow walkway running up the middle, even the biggest of these units has a "cramped" appearance. Although I think it's largely psychological, most owners of pickup campers we've spoken to agree that they're not the thing for extended living—for a trip, say, in excess of three weeks to a month. Many of their owners plan one or two motel stops a week to "stretch out."

If you're considering buying a truck camper, don't forget that you'll need both a truck and the camper unit, and most important, that they *must* be balanced. Trucks suitable to campers come in three ratings: ½ ton, ¾ ton, and 1 ton. Ratings are the key here—don't depend on the length of a truck bed to be an indication of the size of a camper it will carry.

• Half-ton trucks are good only for the lightest campers: camper shells and minimum-convenience cab-over sleepers.

• Three-quarter-ton trucks are the standard for middle-of-the-road campers. Many manufacturers offer "camper specials" in their pickup line, specifically designed to take turtleback homes.

• One-ton trucks handle the biggest units—the kind

that are bolted directly to the truck chassis. They usually incorporate tandem rear wheels to carry the heavy load.

Whenever you match a camper to a truck, here are a few other rules to abide by.

All trucks carry a manufacturer's suggested GVW (Gross Vehicular Weight)—the maximum number of pounds both truck and load can weigh. Never match a camper to a truck if the combined weight of the two exceeds the GVW; you'll ruin the truck, break your bank account buying tires, and end up with dangerous driving problems.

If you're planning on buying a slide-in camper (as opposed to one built on the chassis), don't get one that sticks out further than 12 inches from your lowered tailgate. Excessive overhang puts too much weight on your rear axle and tires, and will result in "fishtailing" as you drive.

Buy heavy-duty tires for the rear end: 6-ply for the lightest campers, 8-ply for a self-contained camper or one with any significant overhang.

MOTOR HOMES

These vehicles have one very pleasant feature. The driver is "home," right under the same roof as the passengers. They can communicate back and forth, and it makes driving and living on the road a lot easier and more pleasant.

Motor homes come in a wide range of sizes just as other recvees do. On the lower end of the size and price scale are the small converted utility vans. Prices on these start at $3,500, and the package usually includes an eating area, beds for from two to four, a built-in icebox, and that's about it. The big, whopping palaces-on-wheels are often built on bus chassis. They include the ultimate in living conveniences and command a correspondingly palatial price—up to $20,000.

The smaller units are the most mobile of all the recvees (with the exception of a four-wheel-drive truck and a camper shell). They can get you up close to hunting and fishing the crowds haven't found, and scoot right along on the open highway. The larger units, because of their great wheelbase and frame, can seldom get off paved roads.

The biggest drawback offered by any motor home is that once your camping vacation is over, you've got something of a white elephant. You can't put it to double duty as a workhorse or second car. Consequently, unless you do a fair amount of wandering in the course of a year, you've got a large investment in cash for a very limited use period.

If you're willing to go small, however, many of the motor vans can be converted back to street use in a day or less. Appliances can be unbolted, and seats—or an open cargo area—left in their place. This is impossible with the larger motor homes; their appointments are permanent. Like truck campers, they also present the "pack it up every time you move" feature, and will trailer a boat.

When you buy a motor home, the same GVW ratings apply to their chassis as to the truck-camper combination. Be sure the weight of the unit doesn't exceed the frame's capacity. And don't forget to figure in passengers, gear, water tanks, food supplies, and so forth when you're tallying up your total weight.

151

CAMPING IN COMFORT

EQUIPMENT FOR COMFORTABLE LIVING

Once you've picked the style of recvee that suits your camping and travel tastes, you'll need to give a lot of thought to size and equipment. Trailers, truck campers, and motor homes not only come in a wide variety of sizes but offer untold options, so where do you begin? Should you buy a big unit or a small one? Should you include air conditioning? Do you need a toilet and shower? How about an oven with your stove? And do you really need a refrigerator when you can save $100 by using an old-fashioned icebox?

Let's begin answering those questions by presupposing two conditions—one that probably doesn't exist in reality. First, let's assume you have an unlimited budget to make your purchase (that's, of course, the debatable condition). Second, although you theoretically have lots of money, you don't want to spend it on unnecessary extras. In short, you can afford a rig that will do the job you have planned for it, but you don't want too much cake frosting.

SIZE. The more room you have to live in, the more pleasant your life will be; there's no debating that. But size will limit where you can go, what you can do, and how much it will cost. A 32-foot trailer, a big motor home, a 12-foot pickup camper mean comfort when you park, but they mean a lot of wind resistance and gas consumption when you drive. You'll be limited to paved roads in top condition.

If you're not too interested in outdoor activity as such, and want an auto camper to see the sights without being

152

chained to motels, restaurants, and reservations, get the biggest unit you can afford.

If you're an indoor/outdoorsman—a guy who likes to wet a line now and then, who likes to see the country that lies beyond the shoulder of the road, but also wants to see the sights and enjoy solid comfort—you'd be wiser to get a medium-sized unit. An 18-to-22-foot trailer, an 8-to-10-foot camper, or a short-wheelbase motor home will still pack plenty of convenience, but will give you a bit more freedom to explore than the large recvees.

Should you be a devoted outdoorsman, the kind of guy who views a camp as a base of operations for hunting and fishing trips, you'll be happiest if your unit will get you into the back country. Only the small, light ones are capable of this function: 10-to-12-foot travel trailers, tent trailers, 8-foot campers, and small utility-van motor homes. They are, of course, short on room and offer minimum comforts.

EQUIPMENT for extensive living should be extensive. If you're planning on using your recvee as a home away from home—planning on using it for months at a time as opposed to week-end or week-long jaunts—all the comforts of home you can cram into its frame will be welcome.

Let's start with those long-period living units. We'll mention the kinds of facilities you'd find welcome on a two-month trip, and then drop down a notch. Those appointments discussed in terms of large homes on wheels would be impractical in the midi-camper and downright foolish in mini-campers, but it doesn't work the other way around. In other words, a stereo tape system would seem a

153

little strange in a soft-top camper trailer, but a dinette wouldn't. And of course, that dinette—or an eating area of some sort—would be mandatory in a large recvee.

• Complete self-containment in a maximum-comfort camper is a must. This means you can live a normal life, free from the tentacles of sanitary hookups and piped-in water and electricity for three days or more. A self-contained unit should have a toilet, shower or bath, hot and cold running water, and at least one 30-gallon holding tank for sewage and one for water.

• A living room or at least living quarters separate from sleeping and eating accommodations

• Air conditioning

• A TV

• A generator system capable of turning out 110 volts

• You might also enjoy the convenience of pint-sized washing machines, driers, and dishwashers.

Medium-sized recvees are suited to a week or two of travel, and during these shorter on-the-road periods, you won't need the extensive appointments of the large recvees. You might, of course, want to incorporate one or two conveniences common to larger units: air conditioning if you do a lot of summer camping down South, or complete self-containment if you'll be traveling the Alcan Highway for example. But aside from these matters of individual taste, here's a rundown on general equipment that should be included:

• Your kitchen should include a pressurized water system, an oven and refrigerator, a fan-driven vent for the stove, and a double sink.

154

• Unless you live in strictly warm climes, you should have thermostat-controlled central heating.

• A toilet—not necessarily incorporating the extra cost of hot water and bathing facilities, but at least a john and a grooming area. These are often arranged so the toilet doubles as a clothescloset, or is hidden under a seat.

THE LIGHTWEIGHTS are best suited to short trips and wilderness wandering. They are available with just the barest essentials, but to our way of thinking, such trimming cuts too far into comfort. We recommend even the smallest units have a permanent stove and icebox, a dinette, a sink and pump-type water system, sleeping for at least three, simple vents on the roof and above the stove, a tie-in for 110-volt electric hookup, and lots of storage space. If you'll be camping in cold weather, a central heating system is a wise investment. If you're not planning on winter camping, a catalytic heater should suffice to keep off the evening chill and damp.

(Our rundown on recvee accommodations doesn't include so-called "camper shells." These amount to nothing more than a bare-walled shelter that fits on a pickup bed. For comfortable living in a camper shell, see the station wagon techniques described in Chapter 4.)

THINGS TO LOOK FOR

Whatever the nature, size, or structure of your camper, there are a few features that every one of them should incorporate.

CAMPING IN COMFORT

The most important is intelligent placing of equipment. Can you reach the refrigerator easily from the stove? The dinette too? Is the sink close to the stove, and does the opening of one cabinet door interfere with the opening of another?

Hand-in-hand with the placing of equipment is the utilization of space. Storage of equipment is one of the biggest considerations in a recvee, so make sure every available space is utilized for either facilities or storage. On truck campers, there should be some kind of access to any dead space in the bed of your truck. On any camper, cabinets and shelves should incorporate some non-slide or nonopening feature: positive, tight-closing locks on cabinets, and fiddleboards (lips that keep shelved things from sliding off) on shelves.

Look for equipment that serves more than one purpose, too, most notably couches by day that are double beds by night, and dinettes that turn down into bunks.

The location of appliances is also important. Look for weight balance. Stoves, refrigerators, water tanks, bathrooms, sinks, and propane tanks are the heavies. They shouldn't all be located on one side or you'll have a hard time driving. On trailers and motor homes, these items should either be evenly distributed around the frame or centered in the middle of the structure. On a trailer, this puts their weight over the wheels. On a motor home, it divides the weight up between the four wheels.

In a truck camper, look for most weight up front, behind the cab. This evens the load out on four tires.

On all recvees, make sure they're built with a stout roof. There's no better place to carry extra gear or a light boat.

There's a simple test for strength you can witness right in the showroom. Ask the salesman to walk on the roof, while you listen inside for the sound of cracking wood or a telltale footprint pressing through the ceiling.

Solid strength should be built into floors too. Check truck campers carefully for this feature. When the camper is at rest in the bed of the truck, it's supported by a perfectly flat surface. But how about when it's off the truck and up on jacks? There's a good chance that you might camp in a permanent spot for a week or so. When that happens, it's worthwhile to remove the camper from the truck so you can do some wandering without breaking camp every time you move. The earth is seldom perfectly flat; if your camper is resting on an uneven surface, without all-around support, will the floor stand up to the strain?

Good insulation is another thing to demand, and make sure floors are insulated as well as walls and roof.

BOTTLED GAS

Most recreational vehicles "live" off bottled gas. It provides the flame for the stove, cools the refrigerator, heats the interior, and even lights the lights when you're not hooked up to electricity.

The best gas to use is liquefied petroleum gas. This is either propane or butane gas under such pressure that it is reduced to a liquid. Propane is the best because it vaporizes or "thaws" at low temperatures.

LP gas is relatively safe to use, and quite efficient. A lot of fuel can be carried in a small space, and it burns

157

with a hot, clean flame. But dependable operation does require a little know-how.

When your tank (or bottle) is filled, there should always be some empty space (about 20 per cent of volume) inside the container. This gives the liquid gas room to vaporize before it enters feed tubes.

For the same reason, any valves or regulators have to be on top of the tank. Usually, that's the only way you can mount them; but mounting screws can work loose, so it pays to be aware of this.

Two tanks are always the best way to go. When one runs out, switch to the other and get your empty filled at the next commercial outlet. That way, you're sure to have a ready supply of fuel. If you don't have the room for two tanks, make sure your single container has some sort of gauge, and keep your eye on it.

Occasionally, the vaporizing gas cools the tank to the point where it will sweat or frost at the level of the liquid. This is something of a "gauge" in itself, but it doesn't happen all the time. Still, it's a handy way to tell if your regular gauge is accurate.

LP gas is great to use, but it presents one problem. Recvees carrying the stuff are prohibited from certain bridges and most tunnels. So if your journey will carry you over or into such places, you'd better make alternate routes a part of planning your itinerary.

SELF-CONTAINMENT

When your home on wheels carries the conveniences of a toilet and bathing facilities, you'll have to empty your holding tanks every few days, and replenish your supply of water.

Most commercial campgrounds include an emptying station as part of their customer package. Many gas stations also boast of this feature, and when they have it, it's usually prominently advertised.

It might be worth pointing out too that bathing facilities use up a lot of water in a very short amount of time. If your family likes to take a shower every day, a 30-gallon tank won't go very far. You might consider installing two such tanks, or plan on water refills every day.

LIVING IN A RECREATIONAL VEHICLE

Living in a recvee comes closer to home than any other kind of camping. You cook your meals just as you do in your own kitchen, sleep on beds with sheets, and eat on a formica table. There's very little camping knowledge needed for a pleasant, comfortable trip. That does not, however, mean there aren't a few tricks to the trade.

• The campsite can be anywhere, and a lot of auto campers overlook this. If you find a particular campground filled, move on to the next and the next. If it's getting late and you want some sleep, and still haven't found an open campground, here are a few other places to look.

The interstate highway system incorporates "rest stops." These are large pull-off areas that contain toilet facilities, phones, drinking water, and sometimes picnic tables. They're good "campgrounds" for an overnight stop.

State highways often have picnic grounds and pull-offs for travelers who want to take a break. While they're seldom as modern as the stops on federal highways, they usually have tables, a garbage can, and occasionally toilets and water. Similar places are often constructed and sponsored in or near small towns by local chambers of commerce. You might also consider city parks, but stop at the police station and check on regulations governing overnight parking first.

When you're near water, don't overlook boatyards. In the summer, land used for winter storage of boats is as empty as a wilderness. Most operators are glad to let you spend the night there, if you'll ask.

In a real pinch, there's also the possibility of supermarket parking lots and just plain roadsides. Again, it might pay to let the local police know your plans.

• Pitching camp involves just one step beyond driving up and parking: you've got to be level. It's surprising, but just a little tilt, hardly noticeable, will result in a poor night's sleep, and some appliances won't work properly unless they're perfectly level either. To learn the angle you're on, you can use a carpenter's level. If you don't carry such a thing around with you, stand a glass of water on a cabinet top or the floor and note the relation of the water surface to the rim of the glass.

If you're tipped, you can do one of three things. You can dig the dirt out from under a wheel or wheels until you're level; you can drive up on a board, rock, or log high enough to get you on an even keel; or you can use a bumper jack to lift a corner of your vehicle into position. The jack method is the best when you plan to stay in one spot for a few days. It gives you a solid floor to walk on, which is a bit more pleasant than the feeling of mushy springs underfoot every time you move around.

• A place for everything and everything in its place is a good rule to follow no matter what kind of camping you prefer. Any kind of recreational vehicle amounts to close living conditions, and clutter has a habit of getting out of hand in a hurry. Make a practice of putting everything away when you're done using it, and really impress this on any children.

• Driving with an auto camper isn't too much different from taking a spin in the family car, but one thing you should be wary of is high winds. A travel trailer, truck camper, or motor home has quite a bit of side area, and this catches wind like a sail. You might not think it possible, but many of these units have literally been blown off the road during a heavy gale. If high winds are predicted for a particular day, you'd be wise to weather them out in camp.

• Many recvees have a disposal system for sink and bathwater that runs directly to the ground outside. If yours has this, make sure you dig some sort of hole to funnel waste liquids into the subsoil (recvee-ers call them "gopher holes").

• Except for the largest travel trailers and motor homes, most recvees don't include laundry equipment. Here's a neat trick that makes washday even easier than the claims of a dozen soap commercials:

Put your dirty clothes in a bucket with a sealed top, add hot water, soap, and hit the road. The vibration of driving will gently clean your washables, so at the end of the day, all you have to do is rinse them out and hang them up to dry.

161

SPECIAL EQUIPMENT FOR THE RECVEE-ERS

There are many pieces of equipment useful to wheeled campers that are seldom included in the package you buy. Some of them are old standards, some brand-new.

• Roll-up boat loaders are a big help if you're car-topping a small craft. They amount to a wide roller, mounted on the end of the roof of your unit. Stand a boat on its stern, leaning against the rear end of your camper or motor home. Pick up the stern and push, and the boat rolls on top of the roof. Rollers not only make nesting your craft easier, they reduce it to a one-man job.

• Smoke detectors—actually detectors for deadly carbon monoxide gas—are a wise companion when you're using heaters in any small airtight area. If dangerous fumes should be present, they sound a loud alarm.

• A small tent isn't a bad investment if you own a recvee. It serves as extra storage space around camp, a plaything that will keep the kids busy outside, and if you have a motor home or truck camper, is sufficient to "hold your campsite" when you want to roam.

• When you're hauling a trailer in the summer, your car will be prone to overheating. If it does—and you've thoroughly checked out the condition and quality of your cooling system—think about a transmission cooler. It's an extra radiator, bolted in front of your present radiator, through which transmission fluid circulates. It helps keep your entire rig a lot cooler. Installation takes two hours, costs run around $70.

• Pickup campers have a door that's quite a step from the ground. Unless you've got long legs, you'll have to include some sort of stepladder for easy entry and exit. Buy one that folds up flush against the outside of your door when not in use. It's hinged right to the camper itself, so all you have to do is pull a pin and it's in place.

• One piece of camper equipment we wouldn't be without is a set of "camper jacks." They attach to the four corners of your unit and fold up out of the way when you're in transit. If you want to drive out from under your home for rugged roaming, swing them down, undo the turnbuckles that anchor your camper to the truck, and jack away. If you don't like to do all that pumping, automatic jacks are made that work with your car's battery.

• Another welcome addition to the pickup camper is an intercom system. If passengers will be riding in the back while you're underway, you'll soon weary of hand signals through the rear window. An intercom system keeps you in touch with whoever is in back of you; it's especially nice to have when there are children along.

• Should trailer camping be your forte, don't forget you'll have to block the wheels when you want to drive away. Special chocks, with rubber tie downs to hold them tightly in place, are the best system we've seen.

• If a mini-motor home appeals to you, you can increase its sleeping capacity by buying one with a special fiberglass roof. These are aerodynamically designed so they don't create wind resistance, and amount to sleeping space for two more. Several manufacturers also offer an optional canvas tent that hooks up to the side door. It's either a full closure or a dining fly.

163

7 Boat Camping

Too many people think a boat is purely a vehicle for traveling across the water. A boat, in fact, is one of the best friends a camper can have.

Once your boat is launched, you have the freedom to go anywhere those waters touch a shore: far to the end of a lake, deep in a maze of estuarine channels, down or up a winding river. And your transportation has the capacity to carry quite a load of comfort along with its passengers.

As a result, a boat means you can get away from the crowds with ease, and without the work and limited comforts that are characteristic of wilderness back- or horse-packing. Just a sampling of the opportunities water-borne campers can count on includes:

• Access to spots never before explored by car campers. With a live-on boat, or any craft packed with canvas, you can see the scenic wonders of the Southwest's Lake Powell, a diamond in the desert. You can explore the shores of the countless Corps of Engineers' water impoundments in the Midwest. In our home state of Montana, we have our own giant lake called Fort Peck Reservoir. It's 180 miles long and has over 1,600 miles of shoreline. Access by car is limited to exactly seven points on the lake shore, but with a boat, every bit of that inland sea beckons the camper.

• The freedom to pick and choose the campsite that suits you best. In the crowded East and on popular tourist-attraction lakes in the West, shoreside campgrounds that can be reached by road are filled to capacity by late morning. Yet the shores of those same lakes only two or three miles away are as empty as any hard-to-get-to back country.

• A unique and rewarding way to take an extended vacation camping trip. Our river systems offer highways of water and unpeopled campsites for anything from an overnight trip to a trip lasting a year or more. An author friend of ours plans to sail his boat around the country just this way. His route includes going up the Hudson River, then west on the St. Lawrence Seaway, across the Great Lakes, and into the Missouri. The Missouri will lead him clear into Montana, where he'll arrange a trailer trip over the Continental Divide and down to the headwaters of the Columbia. From the Columbia, he'll go to the Pacific and poke around for a while, then take another trailer trip from Southern California to the Gulf of Mexico. From then on, it's clear sailing across the Gulf, around Florida, then up the inland waterways of the East Coast to his home in New York.

With a boat, camping equipment, and a lot of time, anyone can "sail around the country."

BOATS FOR CAMPERS

Boats come in a wide variety of designs and dimensions, and some sort of comparison between them and land-locked forms of camping homes might be the best place to begin. There's a world of difference between camping with a mountain tent and camping with a 30-foot travel trailer. They're each suited to very different kinds of leisure activity. The same is true of boats. Each size and style does a particular job best.

There's admittedly a lot of sea between the two extremes of a 6-foot dinghy and the Elizabeth II, but boats for camping do have enough in common to narrow them down to three categories: small open boats, large open boats, and live-on boats.

SMALL OPEN BOATS

This is a relative term. Abbreviated length doesn't have as much to do with it as portability, and this category includes such boats as 16-foot john boats and 21-foot freighter canoes. All the craft that fit here are light enough to be carried on a car-top roof rack, and don't need a monster of an outboard to push them around.

Small open boats are the best choice for the camper who wants a lot of mobility and plans to travel light. They lend themselves to the same kind of fast setup and minimal, functional outfitting common to the quickie camper. They're ideal if your plans include fishing on some hard-to-reach lake where there's no ramp to launch trailered boats, or if you'd like to visit the watery wilderness of places like northern Minnesota or Maine.

The suitable designs for this kind of craft are three: the semi-vee outboard, the john boat, and the canoe.

Semi-vee outboards look like everybody's idea of a "boat." They have a pointed bow, with a bit of a flare to direct

166

spray away from the interior, and a square stern that will take up to a 10-horsepower motor. These are the best boats for general work-horse use: putting around on a small lake, fishing, and ferrying equipment from the launching site to the campsite.

• John boats have a flat bottom and a square, pram-type bow. They're suitable for very small lakes (they're not very good in a chop) and are excellent for floating moderate-to sluggish-moving rivers. They're also roomy craft, very stable fishing platforms, and because of their simple design are the most inexpensive of all the car toppers, costing about $100.

• Canoes are the ideal design if your leanings are toward a more rugged outdoor life. They can take very rough water, and once you learn how, they handle like a precision machine. They're excellent camping boats in that they can handle a huge payload (it takes over 2,000 pounds to sink an 18-footer . . . they'll carry 800 pounds safely . . . while their own weight is feather light, around 100 pounds tops). The best use to put a canoe to is exploring chains of lakes. You can paddle through one lake system, then carry your boat over a hill; or you can shoot the rapids in a river, and drop into a totally new drainage. If you don't like to paddle, canoes will take a small outboard.

CONSTRUCTION. We'll make a blanket statement here: buy aluminum. It's durable, inexpensive, good looking, and most important, light. The complaints we've heard most commonly from anti-aluminum forces are that it's noisy and doesn't stand up in salt water. Unless you're a fishing purist, a little slosh and slap shouldn't offend your senses

167

too much. As to the salt water, that's absolutely right, but we find it hard to imagine anyone taking a tiny car topper out in the ocean, or even in a large bay. If salt water is your leaning, play it safe and get a large boat.

POWER. If you don't want to row or paddle, all these boats will take a small outboard. The best we've run across range from 3 to 5 horsepower with a pivotal reverse. This means that the motor swings 360 degrees. When you want to go in reverse, you simply turn it around in its mounts. A pivotal reverse also means something else—a lighter unit than one with forward-reverse gears, and less cost when you buy.

If you want to put a motor on a canoe, you'll have to use either a special mount so your outboard can hang over the side, or get a square-sterned "guide-model" canoe.

Generally speaking, gasoline-powered outboards are best for most small-boat camping, but on many lakes, most notably those that serve as a water supply for large cities, the use of internal combustion engines isn't permitted. Should you want to boat camp in a place like this, you might consider an electric outboard.

Electric engines run smoothly and quietly, will push a 12-foot car topper loaded with camping gear at 3 to 4 knots, and will run for about 10 hours on a charge. When you tally up the entire unit (engine and 12-volt batteries), the cost and weight of electric are just about the same as a 3-horsepower gasoline outboard.

CAMPING WITH A CAR TOPPER necessitates a camp on shore. They're just too small to live aboard.

Like landlubbers, the small-boat camper should choose

a site away from any obvious dangers and establish his camp on relatively level ground. But unlike land-locked campers, there's a good chance he'll run into two problems common around water: insects and high winds.

The two situations amount to something of a one-or-the-other proposition. If you set up on a breezy point, the wind will keep the insects down but not the camp. Tents will flap, sand will blow, and if you cook over a campfire, you'll have meals spiced with a healthy seasoning of ash.

If you sequester yourself in some protected hollow, morning and evening will fairly buzz with mosquitoes, green flies, black flies, no-see-ums and whatever other brand of insect might be around to bug you.

The best bet for a shoreside camp, then, is a happy medium: a place where the breezes blow, but don't turn into a full gale. Locations like this can usually be found along a straight stretch of shore (as opposed to a point or small bay), with a sparse to medium growth of trees. Pitch your tent back from the shore. If you can get on a little rise—say 10 to 20 feet above the waterline—so much the better as you'll catch the slight breezes that blow morning and evening.

Don't locate on the crest of a dune or hill . . . you're asking to be buffeted from both directions.

Something else to steer clear of in terms of insects is a weedy bay or shoreline. They're bug factories.

• The fireplace. When people pitch camp by the water-side, the temptation is to set the tent back from the water, and place your campfire directly in a line drawn from the tent to the water. If you're camping on a large lake or the sea, don't. In the afternoon, the breeze will blow off the water toward you, carrying sparks and ash right up to your tent walls. Instead, set your fireplace off to one side or the other. It's less smoky and much safer.

Building a fire on some ocean and lake beaches offers another problem—no rocks to line the edge of your fire hole. And when you dig that fire hole, sand keeps falling in to put your fire out.

To solve that problem, beachcomb around and find some heavy, water-soaked logs. You can use them just like rocks, both to line the outer rim of your fire hole and to shore up your shallow fire pit. They should keep your fire where it belongs for quite a while, without burning up themselves.

• Firewood is always easy to find around any shore, but beware of any dimensioned lumber or logs that have been used for pilings or docks. Especially around salt water, wood like this has been treated with a preservative—usually creosote. It burns hot and fast, creating a fire hazard, and gives off a permeating, persistent odor that, even when the wood is reduced to coals, makes food inedible.

• Tenting. If your camp is going to include a canvas tarp for shelter, don't overlook the possibilities of your craft serving as a part of your tent. A canoe, a light outboard, or a john boat all make excellent ridgepoles for elementary canvas homes.

• Packing any boat should be done with care because your safety is at stake. In small car toppers, it's generally agreed that the load should sit squarely in the middle of the craft. Heavy camping gear should go in first and be packed low. This keeps your center of gravity down low where it belongs, so you won't be prone to tip.

Distribute the weight in such a way that when your

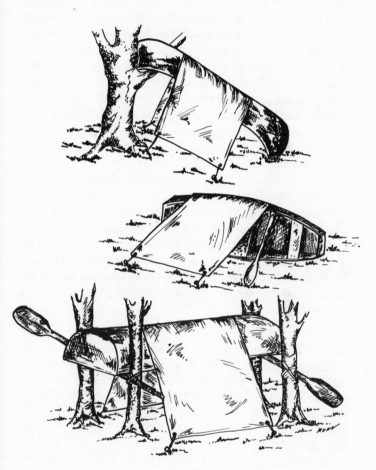

Boat Shelters

boat is full of gear but empty of passengers, it will float on an even keel with no appreciable list to port or starboard, fore or aft. When you're satisfied with your packing, lash the gear in place to prevent weight shifts and the possibility of losing things overboard. You might first cover it with a tarp that can later double as a tent.

Never load a boat beyond its safe limits. The weight capacity will appear on a small metal plate, usually located in the area of the transom. And don't forget to include the weight of your passengers, motor, and gasoline when you're tallying up.

For gear that can be damaged or affected by water (clothing, sleeping bags, cameras, etc.), you might consider the protection of waterproof black rubber dunnage bags. These containers hold as much as a medium-sized suitcase, and can be comfortably carried on your back in the event of a portage. "Black bags," as they're commonly called, can be bought from most large sports stores and mail-order houses, and are occasionally available at shops that cater to boaters.

TRANSPORTING a car topper is logically best on car-top roof racks. The racks should be well padded on top so as not to damage the gunwale of your boat, and have rubber suction cups on the bottom so as not to damage the finish of your car. Tie downs—both those that hold the boat to the rack, and the racks to the car—should incorporate a heavy piece of rubber somewhere in their span. Straight rope or webbing will eventually work loose; rubber keeps tension in and slack out. When choosing a car topper, steer clear of any boat over 150 pounds. More weight than that is a real strain to load. And when your craft is loaded on top of your car, don't overlook the storage space for camping gear that lies inside your overturned boat.

LAUNCHING a light car topper is a snap. Just undo any tie downs, lift it off the rack, and slide it in the water. You don't need any kind of ramp or dockage facilities—that's one of its advantages.

LARGE OPEN BOATS

Large open boats suitable for camping fall between 14 and 18 feet in length. They're too heavy to be carried on roof racks, and must be trailered. While they may have a cabin or canvas shelter, what separates them from live-on boats is a lack of facilities—bunks, a galley (kitchen), and a head (toilet). So you'll have to provide these things by way of bringing tent-camping gear along on your cruise.

These craft are best suited to exploring medium-sized lakes and inland sea waters like bays and estuaries. They don't portage very well, so they're out for wilderness travel, but they do provide a lot of room for passengers and gear. This means you'll be able to pack a lot more comfort into your trip than can be provided by a light car topper.

Large open boats are manufactured in three styles: runabouts, catamarans, and the cathedral or "gull-wing" hull.

• Runabouts amount to a big brother of the semi-vee car topper. They have a pointed bow and square stern, and usually some decking up forward with a windshield. They also have remote controls—you steer and shift by way of a wheel and levers located up front, instead of fiddling di-

173

rectly with your outboard motor. It's a durable design, and the most popular from coast to coast. Since there are so many runabouts floating around, you can pick one up secondhand for relatively little money.

• The catamaran is really two hulls in one. There are two planing surfaces, port and starboard, so when you give her the gas and get up on top of the water, you can see daylight right down the middle. The advantages to this kind of construction are several: (1) you end up with a squarish boat, making more room for people and packing; (2) the boat draws less water, allowing you to maneuver more easily in shallows and close to shore; and (3) it's more stable with less splash in heavy seas. One problem with catamarans, however, is that they need two outboards —one behind each hull. Not necessarily because of power, but because of a thing called cavitation.

• The gull-wing or cathedral hull is the boat we feel hits the top of the mark. This job has a total of *three* hulls— two small ones, port and starboard, and one large one running right down the middle. We don't mean three distinct hulls like boats you may have seen in pictures of the South Sea Islands—just three bulges, all in the same boat, that amount to stabilizing planing surfaces when the boat gets up to speed. Like the catamaran, it's squarish, roomy, and shallow draft, and extremely stable in heavy seas. Unlike the catamaran, it doesn't cavitate and whips along nicely on one engine.

CONSTRUCTION. Aluminum or fiberglass is best for these larger boats. If you know you'll *never* go close to salt water, pick aluminum. Its light weight means easier trailering and

174

handling and less horsepower needed to get it up to speed.

If the ocean or estuaries are your game, get nothing but fiberglass. It's tough, serviceable, and requires no upkeep.

Why not wood? Well, for your very first boat, which should be secondhand . . . maybe. But remember: wood requires a lot of maintenance; and if you trailer a lot, as opposed to dumping her overboard in the spring and hauling her out in the fall, you'll have to cope with strained seams and leaks.

Remember that any non-wood boat will sink without flotation chambers. Make sure your choice has plenty, arranged in such a way that a swamped boat will float rightside up. That means lots of flotation up high—along the rails and under top decking.

POWER. Virtually all used boats and most new ones that fit into the "large-open-boat class" are powered by outboards. This means your engine is a separate unit from your boat. When choosing the horsepower of your engine, remember that you'll get the best performance if you select a motor that will plane your craft—that is, make it skim across the top of the water—when the boat is carrying both campers and their gear. *WARNING*: Never exceed the maximum horsepower recommended by your boat's manufacturer. It will be written on the same little metal plate that lists your load capacity. It's usually located in the stern. If your boat won't plane with the maximum horsepower indicated, it's a sure sign you're overloaded. Get rid of a few campers, make two trips, or get a bigger boat.

Although outboards, as standard power in open boats, have enjoyed a long life and lots of popularity, some day

175

they're going to be old-fashioned. Jet drives are still largely in the experimental stage, but they show great promise for the camping boatman of the future. They work by way of a gasoline engine that drives a strong pump. The pump spews a stream of water out of the stern, pushing the boat just as expanded gases push a jet plane.

The advantages to this kind of propulsion system include a minimum of working parts, a maximum of efficiency and control, and most important, virtually no draft (the amount of water your boat/motor combination needs to float).

At the writing of this book, jet boats are too expensive for anybody but the wealthy (around $8,000 for an 18-footer). But we have seen a 16-foot aluminum runabout in the experimental stage that is planned to sell for around $1,200. The places a boat like this could take the exploring camper are limited by only 3 inches of water, and that takes in a whale of a lot of territory!

CAMPING with a large open boat offers two options: sleeping ashore in a tent or sleeping aboard. Generally, you're limited to the former if your craft is under 15 feet, and have the option of the latter if it's larger than that.

Because open boats don't have live-on facilities, you are, however, obliged to use shore to some extent. You might sleep aboard, but you'll probably have to cook on shore, and set up your eating and living area there as well.

Our own personal preference is for the unencumbered freedom provided by a shore camp when the weather permits. But if sleeping aboard your craft interests you, you might do well to look into the new "convertible" boats manufacturers are now touting. They're the boat camper's dream come true in that they incorporate seats that double as beds, and a canvas tent-like roof all around. In nasty weather, they're roomy and well sealed enough to live in too.

Another possibility open to the camper is the Mossberg Marine Camper. It's a camper trailer that packs a 14-foot runabout for a top. After you back your trailer into an appropriate water-front campsite, the boat flips into the water, and the trailer makes up into a soft-top home that sleeps four adults. You can even buy it with an add-on canvas room if you want to stretch out. Of course with this kind of arrangement, your camp ties you to its shore location and you lose the roam-at-will benefits of more prosaic tent/boat camping.

BEACHING AND MOORING. If you'll be camping in or out of an open boat, you'll have to beach your craft eventually. The procedure's relatively simple. Find a nice, sandy shore and approach it at half throttle. As you near the shore and bottom looms up to greet you, cut your engine and have a passenger tilt it forward so your prop clears the water. You should have headway to drift in.

If you find shoals stretch way out from your prospective campsite, approach shore at the slowest speed your motor will go. When you hear your prop bumping bottom (it's a hard sound to ignore), turn off your engine, swing it clear of the water, and use a set of oars to paddle or pole your way in.

There's always the chance you might want to pull your boat well up on shore, because of an impending storm, or maybe heavy chop pounding the shore. You can slide quite

177

a load up a beach by using round logs for rollers, or wet, slimy wood for skids. If you don't pull your craft well on shore, make sure that you've got a bowline tied to something that won't move easily. There are few things so dispiriting as "missing the boat"—when it's yours and drifting away.

Should your camp plans call for an extended stay on a particular beach, consider building some sort of makeshift dock. They're very wise investments in time and effort in that you won't have to board bow first and climb over windshields or slippery decking every time you want to sail. Just build up a good-sized pile of rocks 20 feet or so from shore, and stretch a log or beachcombed beam from it to land.

When you're camping around salt water, you'll have to plan for tides. The best method is to beach your boat and pitch your camp at high tide. That way you won't have to lug gear between the high- and low-water mark. If you'll want to use your boat within the next ten hours or thereabouts, you'll have to anchor it beyond the low-tide mark. Do this as soon as your gear is unloaded, and plan on doing some wading.

PACKING a runabout gives you a bit more freedom in where you can place gear because the boat is bigger. The rules about weight low, load capacity, and level floating still apply, but you can scatter your camping gear in places where it fits best: in the bow, under seats, under the gunwales, and leave plenty of convenience room for passengers.

When doing that actual loading, it's a much safer and easier job if one camper is aboard stowing gear, and the other one ashore, toting. That way, you eliminate that repeated step from solid ground to floating boat. With an armful of equipment, and the chance of being off balance, that could turn out to be quite a step.

Don't forget that, as you load gear, your boat is drawing more water. This doesn't mean much at a dock, but if you're launching on a lake shore, you'll have to keep pushing the boat into deeper water. There's nothing like getting a boat completely loaded only to find that it's grounded and won't budge. We know—we did it once and had to unload and reload half our gear.

TRANSPORTING an open runabout is largely a matter of trailering. When matching your trailer to your boat, be certain that there is plenty of support for the hull. Trailer supports should meet your boat at points of particular strength: along the chines, along ribs, baffles, and on the keel itself. Make sure there is no stern overhang; if there is, you'll get what's called a "hook" and poor performance. And, of course, you should make quite sure that your trailer is rated for the load your boat places on it.

If you like to get away from it all and explore undeveloped areas, you should choose a trailer with large wheels. Most of them come with wheels that look about right for a tricycle. This is fine for cruising down the paved highway, but those small wheels can give you some problems on a back-country road; they don't want to climb up out of chuckholes too easily, and they lower your axle to the point where it will hang up on the shallowest rut.

A tilt-bed trailer—one that rears up to accept the loading boat—is another good idea if you get off the beaten track

179

a lot. It allows you to launch in shallow water, so you won't be tied to improved ramps.

LAUNCHING. Any trailered boat requires some practice in backing around with that extra set of wheels before you tackle a crowded ramp (see "Driving with a Trailer" in Chapter 2).

Once you're reasonably sure you can coax your trailer to go where you want it to, pull up to the ramp, get into a backup position, and get out from behind the wheel. First, check your boat's drain plug. Is it in place? I'm *always* forgetting to do this and I'm now at the point where I don't even get embarrassed when I have to jump aboard and get the thing in its hole before my boat sinks. I'm even learning how to bail right then and there with a degree of dignity.

Next, undo any and all tie downs except the snap attached to your cable winch. Secure a bowline so your boat won't float away, and if you have a tilt-bed trailer, pull the pin that holds it in the horizontal position.

Back the trailer completely into the water. In order for your boat to float free, you'll probably have to ease your rear bumper right up to the water's edge. Unsnap the winch cable and give a hard shove. Your boat should roll right on in. If it doesn't, you're not backed far enough into the water, or you're not putting enough muscle behind your shove. Try both solutions.

HAULING your boat out of the water requires a bit more doing. The boat must approach the trailer in a straight line with the trailer tongue, so that the keel lines up perfectly with its bed. Make sure your winch cable is unwound and ready to snap into place.

Getting everything lined up isn't too much of a problem on a calm day, but wind can blow you off course with maddening ease. If you're greeted by this plague, try a stern line, held by a shoreside sailor, to steady you.

Ease the boat as far onto the trailer as it will go under its own power, turn off your engine, snap the cable in place, and crank away. When the boat is bedded, haul it out of the water, but don't drive off.

Check to make sure the hull is resting comfortably on all points of support, and in line with the trailer. Cinch up any tie downs and replace the tilt-bed pin if your trailer has this feature. You might also pull the drain plug to get rid of any accumulated water. *Now* you're ready to go on your way.

LIVE-ON BOATS

Large craft for campers amount to a seaside counterpart of motor homes. They're a floating camp with lots of comfort and convenience aboard. These boats are usually no smaller than 16 feet, and can go up to 60-foot yachts. For our purposes, though, let's limit the size to boats that can be trailered. And, yes, we've seen 40-footers tooling down the highway, but unless you've got a semi-tractor parked in your garage, 24 feet is about all you'll be able to handle. And even then, you've bitten off quite a hunk.

Boat designs for living aboard come in two kinds: the houseboat and the sea skiff. Houseboats that can be trailered are relatively new on the camping scene. Because of legal requirements, they can't have more than an 8-foot beam, and because of trailering problems, can't exactly match up to the comforts of the 30- and 40-foot floating palaces that are becoming common to America's waterways.

But even with their limited space, a 24-foot houseboat offers at least as much convenience as an equivalent-sized travel trailer, and—perhaps most attractive—it can be lived in when it's on the trailer or in the water.

Houseboats are best for the boatman who plans to sail in protected waters, to explore the Mississippi, poke around the shores of a medium-sized lake, or stay within the confines of bays and channels. They simply can't take the heavy water that often builds up on our oceans and Great Lakes. Because of their boxy construction, they can pack double the comforts, equipment, and passengers of an equivalent-sized sea skiff.

The price of this kind of craft will fall between $5,000 and $10,000 depending on the optional equipment you buy, and the power plant you select. The wise houseboatman picks a product that planes—a craft that can lift itself up out of the water and scoot along at speeds around 15 knots or better. This not only means you'll be able to get where you're going in a hurry; it's something of a safety margin should you be out on big water when a storm builds up.

Perhaps the most innovative trailerable houseboats we've seen incorporate trailer, boat, and living accommodations all in one unit. When you're ready to go into the water, wheels either retract into the hull, or pontoons are lowered hydraulically. There are no problems getting your camping home on or off a trailer—and with a boat that can weigh

182

up to 5,000 pounds, those problems can be considerable. It's a bit far out right now, but we predict that within the next ten years, someone is going to figure out how to hook up the boat's engine to a set of houseboat retractable wheels, and market an amphibious motor home!

Choosing a sea-skiff design in your live-on boat means you'll be able to handle big water—even up to the ocean itself. But don't tackle that until you've got a good pair of sea legs under you.

Because of the necessary water-shedding design of a sea skiff—a pointed, flared bow; a lot of low decking; and scuppered cockpits—they don't afford the room and, consequently, the extensive comforts of an equivalently sized houseboat. They're work horses, and better suited to the active water sportsmen than to casual campers who want to cruise the inland countryside in water-cushioned comfort. A comparison between a houseboat and sea skiff would come close to the same differences and advantages that can be found between a minimum-comfort truck camper and a large motor home.

Although the difference between a 24-foot "sportfisherman" and the same length houseboat is a big one, to our way of thinking, both should incorporate certain minimum conveniences. In a nutshell, they are:

• A large, open (or canvas convertible) deck area. Whatever your outdoor persuasion—fisherman, water skier, sun bather, or captain of a cruise—you'll enjoy your boat a lot more if you have plenty of room to move about in the open air.

• A galley, complete with cooking, refrigeration, and washing facilities. Your stove should be LP gas or alcohol.

183

CAMPING IN COMFORT

Never use white-gas stoves or lights on a boat, and steer clear of non-permanent LP-gas units, the stoves, lights, and heaters you use while tenting. Unless they're secured in some sort of permanent mount, the rock of the boat could tip them over with disastrous results. Ideally, your stove should be mounted on gimbals—a hinge-like affair that keeps your stove stable while the boat rocks. There should also be a venting system over your stove for cooking odors and heat.

• A dual electric system capable of handling 12 volts from your engine battery and 110 volts when you tie up at a marina.

• A self-contained toilet. All new boats are required to have this kind of head by law. Some old ones don't. If you buy secondhand and see your sewage will dump directly into the water, get it changed, please! Our waters are polluted enough as it is.

• A dinette. Your eating area is most convenient when it's within short reach of your galley facilities. Look for dinettes that make into bunks by night for space economy.

• Bunks that serve more than one purpose, like the aforementioned dinette. Other functions we've seen them perform include: couches, closets, pilot seats, and rope lockers. You might also make sure that when the bunks are set up, they don't interfere with traffic through passageways, particularly the route between bed and head.

• Lots of storage space. Boating requires quite a few accoutrements such as life jackets, ropes, buckets, fire extinguishers, fenders, and most likely, fishing gear. Add them to the normal collection of goods required for an extended trip, and you have quite a ponderous pile of stuff to put away.

CONSTRUCTION. Manufacturers use steel, aluminum, and fiberglass to build these large craft, but we lean toward fiberglass as an all-around material. Just because you get a fiberglass boat, however, doesn't mean you're home free. Make sure your boat manufacturer knows something about marine design, not just how to make a boat look pretty. Check for thickness of the hull material—lots of layers of cloth heavily impregnated with resin. No fiberglass surface should give to the hand, no matter how hard you push. There should be plenty of reinforcement at stress points: the bow, the keel, on the stern quarters and the transom, and anyplace one boat part joins another (cabin to deck, deck to hull, etc.). Look, too, for stout ribbing and baffling, and a drainage system that allows passage of accumulated water to the lowest portion of the hull, where it can be pumped out.

Should you decide on a metal hull of some sort, make sure it's well protected against corrosion. With steel, this means sandblasted inside and out, and painted with epoxy. On aluminum, an anodic type of corrosive preventive is needed to prevent electrolysis in salt water.

POWER. Inboard/outboards are a relatively new item on the boating market, and delightfully suited to the combination camper/trailer sailor. Their power comes from an inboard motor, permanently installed in the stern of your craft. The motor drives a propeller, mounted on the outside of your transom, that looks like the lower half of an outboard motor, hence the name "inboard/outboard." The advantage of this kind of power plant is inboard dependability and convenience with outboard latitude. The "outboard" part of the system can be tilted up via hydraulic motors so the prop is barely scraping the water. This allows tremendous flexibility both in launching and cruising in very shallow water.

Straight outboards rate a bland "O.K." in smaller live-on boats, but generally don't perform as well or as satisfactorily as inboard/outboards. Since they're usually mounted in some sort of well, they also take up valuable space in larger craft.

Pure inboards with a fixed driveshaft and propeller are out for trailering. They require very sophisticated launching pads to get them into the water, and only large marinas have them.

"Camping" on a large, live-on boat requires only one thing —the toss of an anchor. Choose a spot that's well protected. On large, open water, look for a bay or cove. Settling down there means you won't have to worry about tossing and rolling if a storm comes up in the night.

If you're cruising down (or up) a river, find a spot out of the main current. Even in this situation, you'd be wise to look for a protected lee. Locating off the beaten track means you won't be bothered by the wakes of ships that pass in the night, or the danger of a collision. Along those same lines, always be sure that you haven't inadvertently set up camp in a channel or main thoroughfare.

Once your anchor is out, if there's any breeze at all your boat will "yaw"—swing from side to side on its anchor cable. If yawing bothers you while you sleep, you can toss a second anchor out of the stern and it will keep you in one position all night long.

If you plan to anchor overnight, don't forget that you must have one white light, plainly visible from all quarters, that will burn through the night. It's the law as well as a safety measure.

And while we're on the subject of safety, it's also a good idea to leave a length of rope hanging over the stern when you're riding at anchor. That way a man overboard will have something to hold on to.

TRAILERING a big boat requires big, heavy-duty trailers. They should incorporate the tilt-bed feature, have at least four wheels, and a braking system of their own—usually electric brakes that hook up to your car's brake pedal. If your boat is over 2,000 pounds, you should also include an electric winch on your trailer. It will wind your boat up onto the trailer bed all by itself, and will save you a lot of hard labor and frustration.

WATER SAFETY

Whatever the size of your camping craft, two things account for your safety on the water: you and your equipment. Since your equipment should be on board before you, let's take a look at that first.

SAFETY EQUIPMENT. Coast Guard-approved life jackets for everyone aboard are a must—and the law. Make sure they're kept in a place where they can be reached fast in an emergency, not stowed under several hundred pounds of camping gear.

• A fire extinguisher is next on the list. They're not too necessary if you're paddling a canoe, but you need one if you have any kind of permanent gas tank, if you store your portable gas tanks in an enclosed area, or if you have an installed electrical system (electric starter-motors, and running light hookups as opposed to flashlight battery running lights).

• A life-ring and rope. Should a man go overboard, he'll have something to cling to and you'll have something to pull him aboard with.

• A bilge pump. There's quite a bit of latitude in what constitutes a bilge pump here. For instance, we find a sponge and cut-down Chlorox bottle plenty of bail-power for our 14-foot john boat. We use a hand-operated portable pump and a bucket for our 16-foot runabout. We once had a 30-foot cabin cruiser, and didn't feel comfortable until we had two pumps put in, one electric, one hand operated.

• An anchor with 100 feet of rope is a minimum requirement for any open-water craft. It's also wise to put about 6 feet of chain between your anchor and your rope to prevent the rope from cutting and wearing out. On larger boats that venture far out into open water, carry two anchors with ropes. On the aforementioned 30-foot cruiser, we carried *three* anchors—one of them a canvas "sea anchor" or drogue—in case we had to fight heavy storms at sea.

Although that's the core of safety equipment, here are a few other items you might want to consider. They're not just for safety—they also make your boating and camping a lot more pleasurable.

• A first-aid kit. You've got one for your camp, but get a second one and keep it aboard your boat.

• Extra rope. It has a hundred uses ashore and afloat.

• A stay-on-board bucket

• Oars or paddles. Even on a large boat, they're handy for maneuvering in tight places.

• A portable radio, to hear of impending storms

• A compass. Fog or heavy rain can get you lost in a bucket.

• A boat hook

• A boat ladder

• Boat fenders

• Life preservers that can be worn like clothes. Many boaters are reluctant to wear bulky standard preservers, even if they can't swim. These new sport-vest and jacket-type preservers are good looking and stylish, and now have Coast Guard approval. You can't even tell they're preservers, and they work for women and children too.

SAFETY PRACTICES AFLOAT. Like driving on the road, it pays to watch out for the other guy when you're on the water, but don't look in his direction alone. Statistics prove the greatest threat to personal safety on any kind of water is none other than you.

To cut down the odds you've got stacked against yourself, and to ensure that all your water-borne camping trips will be safe, happy ones, make sure every nonswimmer and child is wearing a life jacket before he gets on board. Even if you have an 11-year-old who can swim like a fish, better make him wear a jacket anyway. Most states rule that children under 12 must wear them.

CAMPING IN COMFORT

Another thing to watch is overloading. We talked a little about rated safety limits on boats—engine power and load capacity. Remember that load capacity assumes *normal* conditions. We've found that there's seldom such a thing as "normalcy" around the water—especially large bodies of water. Storms can whip up in the twinkling of an eye on Wyoming's Jackson Lake. Around the famed beaches of New York's Long Island, sea breezes of up to 20 knots can be counted on every summer afternoon. So play it safe. Unless you're camping on a very small lake or floating on a sluggish river, use that overload rating as an undesirable maximum, and go light.

Weather is another consideration. Sure, any camping trip runs the risk of a rainstorm, but if the forecasters call for heavy winds and squalls the day you plan to leave, postpone your outing for 24 hours.

It also pays to be something of an amateur meteorologist yourself—especially in the case of great, anvil-headed clouds that build into thunderstorms on sultry days. This weather condition is extremely difficult for the weatherman to predict in terms of strength and the area it will hit, so you'll be largely on your own.

Be particularly watchful on days with a lot of haze, hot temperatures, and no wind. Keep your eye on great, puffy cloud formations called cumulus clouds. If they start to build up and join together, and develop a dirty-gray coloration on their bottom side, stay off the water.

It's also a good idea to stay reasonably close to shore at all times. Admittedly, the shortest distance between two points is a straight line, but an extra gallon of gas burned for the longer route is a small price to pay for the comfort of a shoreline that's a stone's throw away.

When you're under way, make sure everybody stays seated, and try to place your passengers as you stowed your gear—with weight evenly distributed. Because some items of camping gear can have sharp edges and corners, make sure you've packed them so they can't come in contact with shinbones or feet.

Always handle your boat safely and prudently. Don't make sharp turns—even if you don't turn your boat over, you'll throw your passengers off balance. Don't cut close to buoys, rocks, or other boaters, and steer well clear of swimmers and water skiers.

RULES OF THE ROAD

Boaters don't have the advantage of things like white lines painted down the middle of the water, curbing, and traffic lights. But traveling the waterways isn't just a matter of helter-skelter, by-guess-and-by-gosh either. There are a few accepted rules of the road that govern where you should go and who is in the right.

Imagine your boat is split into quarters—one line running down the middle of the keel, the other cutting your boat in half from port to starboard. If you see a boat approaching from the right-hand front quarter (seasoned salts call it "from dead ahead to two points abaft the starboard beam"), that boat is the "privileged vessel." It has the right of way.

In a narrow channel, boats approaching from opposite

directions pass portside to portside (left to left) just as on the road. When you're passing from behind in a channel, pass on the left, again, just like driving a car. When you're in open water, you can pass on either side. However, in any overtaking situation, you're the burdened vessel. That means it's up to you to watch out for the other guy.

Never anchor in a channel, and never anchor in such a way that you might obscure a buoy. Even though you might be the privileged vessel, give any large boat the right of way. Let's face it, it's a little presumptuous to expect an ocean liner to get out of the way of an 18-foot runabout.

Should your camping trip take you up or down a river, the boat going upstream is the burdened vessel. He has to steer clear of any craft coming with the current, because the boat going upstream has more control.

Buoys. The key to understanding buoyage is a bit of alliteration that goes "red, right, return." When you're leaving a port, it's assumed you're going to the sea. The red buoys will be on your left, black on your right. When returning to port, you're proceeding from the sea—returning—and red buoys will be on the right.

Realize that, because of local variances, this is at best a rule of thumb, at least in terms of where the "sea" is. But after you pass two buoys or more, you should have an idea of where to go, because buoys are progressively numbered, and decrease in their numerical value as you get closer to the sea. When the buoys you pass run from 30 to 1, keep the red on the left. When they run the opposite way, keep the red on the right because you're supposed to be returning from the sea.

CHARTS. Nautical charts are a bit like road maps. They show you water depths, obstructions, buoys, channels, ports, and the like. Charts are available for any waters used for commercial transportation and can usually be obtained from one of three agencies: the Coast Guard, the Army Corps of Engineers, or the Conservation Department of the state in which you plan to sail. Even if these people don't have them on hand, they can put you in touch with agencies that do.

NAVIGATION. There's a great deal of both know-how and equipment connected with accurate navigation—so much that it would take a book twice this size to just scratch the surface. But here is an elementary means of navigation that's pulled us out of a few foggy spots. It requires nothing more than a compass, a watch, and a knowledge of your water speed. (An "aquadometer"—a boat speedometer—can be installed in your craft to take the guesswork out of your water speed.)

First, get an idea of how fast your craft is going.

Next, pay attention to your compass readings and the time it took to cover any particular heading. For example, you might note that you ran for half an hour at 18 knots on a due-south heading, fifteen minutes at 18 knots on a south-by-southeast heading, and so forth.

Should you get caught in a fog or heavy rain that obscures buoys and shores, all you have to do is reverse your readings, and you're bound to find your way back to camp, marina, boatel, or home port.

When we did a lot of ocean cruising, Sil kept regular lists of our headings and speeds to places most frequented. One of those places was a sunken wreck off the Long Island coast. It was great fishing for a variety of salt-water species, and we'd often sleep overnight, right above the wreck.

One week end, we awoke to a pea-soup fog that made us feel as if we were inside a frosted glass ball. There was no definition to anything—the water melted into the sky, and the farthest we could see was about 20 yards.

We tried sitting it out, but by two in the afternoon, we decided it wasn't going to clear and that we'd better give our navigation system the ultimate test. It worked amazingly well, so well, in fact, that after exactly an hour and a half of running, we hit the bell buoy at the head of the Fire Island inlet right on the button, and threaded our way through the channel into protected waters.

CAMPGROUNDS

Like landlubbers, boaters can count on the conveniences of state and federal campgrounds. They're quite common on popular United States waterways and vacation spots that boast lots of water.

There's a great degree of similarity between auto campgrounds and boat campgrounds, including the fact that they're packed by noon during the heavy-use months.

While many of these shoreside facilities can be reached by car, there are a few campgrounds that can only be floated to. These are undoubtedly the most pleasant for the boat camper, if for no other reason than that the crush of company is a little less than those facilities that attract both boats and autos.

Commercial campgrounds for the boat camper are also available, only they're not called campgrounds at all. They're known as . . .

MARINAS. These places amount to a safe-haven port, complete with mooring and dockage facilities that charge dockage fees. The better marinas offer electrical and water hookups for your craft, a sewage-dumping station, and such shoreside amenities as picnic tables, fireplaces, barbecue grills, and swimming pools. They also sell gasoline, oil, ice, and boast of a fair selection of boating equipment.

Marinas often include boatels—a kind of motel built right next to the water. So if you yearn for a bed that doesn't rock, you might want to spend a night or two in one of these. They're usually set up so you can dock your boat a few feet from your front door.

Remember, however, that marinas and boatels are commercial campgrounds in another way. At the height of the boating season, they're often filled to capacity early, so plan ahead and make a reservation.

RENTALS

Boat camping gear can be rented just like any other brand of outdoor living equipment. Should wilderness wandering be your forte, canoe outfitters working at the edge of the Quetico-Superior canoe wilderness in northern Minnesota will set you up with a craft, maps, packs, sleeping bags, and even plan your freeze-dried meals. Many areas in Maine boast of the same services.

If larger boating interests you, rental services exist on virtually every large body of water in the United States. They'll rent you a floatable outdoor home for from $150 to $250 a week, plus gas. But make sure you let them know about your plans early in the year. Their boats are usually all booked up for the season by the end of April.

195

8 Gypsy Camping at Home and Abroad

Did you ever have romantic dreams about joining a band of roving gypsies and saying good-by to bill collectors, Saturday lawn mowers, and predictable tomorrows? To visit faraway places with unpronounceable names? If you're a camper, that dream is just a few steps away from reality, because there's no better way to travel abroad as well as at home.

Most people who camp their way through foreign countries decide to do it that way because they know they'll save money. There's no debating that fact. Figure a camping trip through any country will cost you just about half of what a hotel tour-type trip would. But there's a lot more to be gained than cash savings alone. There's a world of people to meet, already acquainted with you because you share the common denominator of camping. A world of discovery, unfettered by the apron strings of tour guides. A world of sights, sounds, and experiences that you're a part of . . . not just a visitor to or observer of.

In practical terms, camping in a strange land is essentially like camping anyplace. Your home is where you pitch your tent or park your trailer. But beyond the campsite itself, there are a few unique requirements that will have to be met in individual countries, as well as unusual conditions you should know about and plan for.

Perhaps it's a case of putting the cart before the horse, but maybe we should first examine those "faraway lands" that account for the two most recent stars on our flag: Alaska and Hawaii.

ALASKA

At first glance, our largest state would appear to be a camper's oyster. Lots of open, public land, fishing and hunting that make a sportsman's eyes pop, and magnificent scenery. All those outdoor opportunities are there all right —the problem is you can't get to them very well by road.

Virtually all of Alaska's road system lies between the two main cities of Fairbanks and Anchorage. Access to other parts of Alaska is geared to plane travel. Period. And although we confidently predict the day of the amphibious motor home, we doubt we'll live to see them fly.

But even with Alaska's limited roads, the places a camper can drive to still amount to quite a patch of earth, so don't think we mean to sound discouraging about Alaska—just practical.

Getting to Alaska to *go* camping offers yet another problem. You can drive on up over the Alcan Highway, a 2,000-mile-long swath of gravel that's eaten up more than one new tire. You can sail your rig up to Anchorage by way of the inland passage and a commercial ferry service out of Seattle, Washington. Or you can fly into either Anchorage or Fairbanks and rent a camping outfit there.

Should you decide to make use of your own equipment all the way, here are a few things to remember before you pack your bags.

• Tenting is largely out. High winds, low temperatures, lots of rain, and a surfeit of insects make camping under canvas a job for Indians, Eskimos, and survival schools. About 90 per cent of the recvees in Alaska are truck campers, and they are undoubtedly best suited to handling this state's rugged camping conditions.

• Vehicles should be equipped with two spares. Of the roads that exist, many are two-way, black-top highways, but there are enough gravel cowpaths to justify this extra precaution.

• Driving on these gravel roads should be slow. Thirty-five mph is a sensible average. This saves wear and tear on your tires and running gear, as well as on you. When a car approaches, it's a good idea to slow way down so you or he won't kick up flying gravel. Broken windshields and headlights are commonplace occurrences. Always make sure that everything—gas, propane, oil, water—is three fourths or more full before you pass a gas station. Service stations are often few and far between. If you have road trouble, don't walk for help. Wait for a passing motorist and flag him down. Ninety-nine times out of a hundred he'll give you every assistance within his power.

• Camping in Alaska boasts of a few quirks too, and the strangest is that drinking water is in short supply. There are plenty of running streams, but glacial silt makes their

198

waters unpotable. It's even undesirable stuff to wash clothes and dishes in.

Campgrounds don't offer much in the way of the luxury you're used to in the other 48 continental states. The best have picnic tables, a garbage can, and a graveled place to park. Drinking water at a campground is unusual enough for its existence to be mentioned specifically in state campground directories. At home, its presence is expected and accepted without mention.

Understandably, the best time to visit Alaska is during the height of the summer—the last two weeks of July and the first two of August. At this time, plan clothes for a temperature range that runs all the way from 90 to 40 degrees.

HAWAII

Few places are better suited to the tent camper than Hawaii. Temperatures are consistently mild, rainfall practically on a time-clock schedule, and the whole population is oriented to outdoor living.

Obviously, you can't drive there. You can have your family car shipped over by freighter, but we think a more practical solution is to rent a car while you're there. Rental prices are only slightly higher than on the mainland, and you'll more than make up for the extra cost in the hotel bills you'll save. With weight limits on aircraft far more liberal than they used to be, it's quite possible to carry a goodly portion of your camping gear as part of your baggage. What you can't bring, buy there.

199

CAMPING IN COMFORT

Public campgrounds exist on all but the two smallest of the Hawaiian Islands, so you can plan on doing some island-hopping as well. Most of the facilities are federal, state, or civic, and amount to improved public campgrounds. They lack the luxurious facilities of large commercial establishments, but with Hawaii's temperate climate and abundant water, who needs things like swimming pools and hot showers?

CANADA

Crossing over the border to visit our closest neighbor should really be the first step for any family planning on a foreign country camp out.

Canadians are friendly, the majority of them speak a language we understand, and their customs and mannerisms are close to ours. But still, when you cross that imaginary line that separates two countries, and see a maple-leaf flag in place of the red, white, and blue, you're going to experience a bit of culture shock. We're not saying it's bad, or even uncomfortable. In fact we think it's a healthy, educational experience. But that feeling is there nonetheless, and like a shakedown cruise before a long vacation, it's a good idea to get your feet wet with a short trip before you dive in with a long one across the sea.

Camping in Canada is just like camping in the good old U.S.A. Canadian campgrounds boast of the same facilities and campground layouts you left back home. Often they're even better. Many of them include a kitchen compound for indoor cooking. They have commercial campgrounds too, many of them owned by U. S.–based corporations, and public campgrounds (called provincial instead of federal or state).

As a rule of thumb, you can count on the number of available developed Canadian campgrounds to be directly proportional to their proximity to the United States. Southern Canada has plenty of them, particularly Southeastern Canada, where they're frequented by campers from our great eastern megalopolises.

As you get farther north, however, their frequency and the extent of their facilities begin to dwindle. The Northwest Territories, for example, a huge piece of real estate larger than Alaska, has only ten developed campgrounds.

If your plans include the far Canadian North, figure on conditions comparable to camping in Alaska.

Border-crossing into Canada doesn't involve much red tape. Don't bring any sidearms as they're illegal throughout the country. To get back into the United States, you'll need proof of your citizenship. A birth certificate is best. Driver's license and Social Security card aren't acceptable. As in all foreign countries, make sure you're covered by appropriate auto insurance.

MEXICO

As in Canada, the facilities for campers decrease the farther you get from the United States. So does the relative quality of the roads, so if you're planning a trip deep into the interior, consider using a heavy-duty vehicle: a van, panel truck, or pickup.

CAMPING IN COMFORT

Mexicans haven't really kept pace with the camper influx into their country, and campgrounds, as such, are virtually non-existent. If you want to camp next to neighbors, consider renting a plot at a trailer park. There are a few of these operations around.

Driving in Mexico is a lot like driving at home, except for the large number of animals and pedestrians wandering around on the roads. For that reason, it's a good idea not to do a lot of night driving. You might also be wary of narrow, one-way bridges, common throughout the country. They're a first-come, first-served kind of thing, and Mexican drivers often race to see who'll get there first.

Gasoline is sold through a government-owned petroleum company, Pemex. Occasionally, high octane—the gasoline needed by the high-powered Detroit monsters—isn't readily available. The two inferior grades of gas—Gasolmex and Supermex—are sold in most large towns, and work well enough in garden-variety automobiles.

For your border crossing, you'll need proof of vaccination within the last three years, and your birth certificate. You must pick up a tourist card at the Mexican consulate nearest your border crossing. While you're there, you might also inquire about Mexican insurance for your car. Most American insurers don't cover you while you're in foreign countries, and we know a couple who got into a whale of a legal bind over an accident in Mexico.

Aside from the normal practices of planning ahead for your stops, and having a good idea of where you're going and how long it will take, here are a few more things you should consider when camping south of the border.

• Take plenty of water along. Don't depend on local water unless you purify it first. Even avoid local bottled drinks, and remember ice is made from water. A particularly good solution to the water problem for the recvee-er is to have a water purifier and filter installed as part of the self-contained water system. With this setup, you can drink virtually any water, so long as you draw it from your own tap.

• You can eat the local vegetables if they're thoroughly cooked. Avoid raw vegetables and fruits.

• Have a well-detailed map of the area you plan to travel, and learn in advance what the Spanish-language road signs mean.

• Treat the local people as if you were a good-will ambassador—you are. A good friend of ours always takes some old clothes, cooking utensils he no longer needs, and candy on his camping trips. He's made many friends and had some unique adventures in payment for his kindness.

CENTRAL AND SOUTH AMERICA

Camping out in the southern reaches of our hemisphere is for the adventurous. There are virtually no developed campgrounds or camping facilities in any country but Brazil. Transportation is another problem; few countries are connected by roads.

If this kind of adventure interests you, you'll need a passport and a visa for any country you'll be visiting. You'll also need a considerable amount of camping experience under your belt.

CAMPING IN COMFORT

EUROPE

Camping is a way of life throughout Europe, not just a leisure activity as it is in the United States. As a result, there's no better way to see the Old World economically and comfortably.

All the large cities—Paris, London, and Rome to name a few—have campgrounds close to their centers. Campers are often better situated than travelers who stay in the most expensive hotels. Campgrounds are clean and modern too, with tasteful settings and most of the facilities you've come to expect of stateside campgrounds.

CUSTOMS AND ENTRY throughout most of Western Europe are relatively simple. You'll need a U. S. passport, but generally won't need a visa. Officials are characteristically friendly toward U. S. campers, and it's a sure bet they'll be more interested in your camping gadgetry than contraband. Before entering any country, however, it pays to know what you can and can't carry across the border. In general, firearms are out. Large supplies of liquor or tobacco, or a mountain of gifts for family and friends back home, will be subject to import duties.

MONEY should be carried in small-denomination traveler's checks. That way you won't take too much of a beating from foreign exchange rates. Always try to cash them in banks for the same reason. Don't plan on using personal checks—they're virtually impossible to cash.

CREDIT CARDS are catching on in Europe, but their acceptance isn't so universal that you can throw away your traveler's checks. American Express, Carte Blanche, and Diner's Club are the most popular.

CAMPING GEAR for a pleasant European trip amounts to the same equipment you've learned to love back home. There are one or two little twists that you should be aware of, however.

• Don't bring white-gas stoves or lanterns. White gas is often hard to find. Use propane for fuel; it's popular all over Europe.

• Electrical hookups will be 220 volts, so you'll need an adapter for your American appliances, if you don't want to buy their equivalents there.

• Tables and benches are an uncommon luxury at European campsites, so consider bringing camp chairs and card table along.

• Portable campstoves are a must. Campfires are seldom permitted.

• Europe's climate is a lot like the East Coast's—they have ample rainfall and their share of chill temperatures. Norway could be compared to Maine, Holland to New York City, Southern Spain to Florida. Match your clothing to your destination. Generally, informal dress is accepted in Europe for most situations. Europeans have not yet gotten used to the idea of slacks and shorts on women for street wear, which seems a bit strange in view of the mini-kinis you'll see at the beaches there.

• Should you plan to buy your camping gear in Europe, you'll find the prices reasonable and the quality excellent. Most of it is the sparse-convenience kind of stuff used by back-packers and mountaineers. Tents often have no floors or bug screening, and are on the small side. One- and two-burner stoves are popular, three-burner stoves hard to find. If you find you really like some feature of your own camping gear—say the roominess of an extended and compartmental umbrella tent you own—bring it with you.

Campgrounds are common throughout Europe. They're usually indicated on road maps, or can be located by a listing published by each country's tourist information bureau. Frequently, these listings are a border-crossing handout.

In order to be admitted to most European campgrounds, you'll need a camper's carnet—a card that's a bit like our federal "recreation passport." They're usually sold right in the campground; in this country, they can be bought through AAA.

As in the United States, most countries rate their campgrounds by a system of stars or numbers so you can get an idea of the facilities to expect. They usually include stores, washing and toilet facilities, and a tent area. Rates for the best campgrounds can go as high as $3.00, but the average you can expect to pay is around $.80.

Camping on private land is also common, particularly in Britain, but you must get the owner's permission first. And if he gives it (which he probably will), offer to tip him. If you want to build a fire, ask him first. Some countries don't permit open fires in wooded areas, and European campers in general aren't quite so tied to the crackle of a campfire as their American cousins. Consequently, permission to camp and permission to build a fire are two quite separate subjects.

206

CAMPING in most countries of Western Europe is just like home—including the fact that campgrounds are usually filled early during the height of the summer camping season.

The two most popular forms of camping homes are tents and small motor homes. The Volkswagen "campmobile" heads the motor home popularity poll.

The campsites themselves are a bit on the small side by American standards, but like the neat, close houses of Amsterdam and Paris, a fellow camper within reaching distance is part of the charm of it all.

You'll find that European campers are extremely courteous too. They'll be mouse-quiet when it's getting close to bedtime, and expect you to be the same.

Theft around campgrounds is virtually non-existent. There's an exquisite code of honor among European campers. But it does occasionally happen on the road— especially in the larger cities of Southern Europe. If you're using a motor home or trailer, make sure everything is under lock and key if you leave for a while to take in the sights.

Drinking water in the northern countries is relatively safe. In the south, you'd be wise to purify it in some way. When it comes to cooking, you'll save a lot of money if you prepare meals that fit right in with the local diet. Besides being inexpensive and available, native foods are all part of the total experience of living in another country.

You'll also save the most money if you buy fresh foods as opposed to frozen or canned goods. Small towns are still short on refrigeration and ice, so most of Europe is geared to daily shopping in green groceries.

When you're shopping or around camp, you might run

207

into a few language difficulties. A surprisingly large number of Europeans speak some English, so the barriers won't be so great as to be insurmountable. You might, however, invest in a phrase book for each country you plan to visit, and polish up your sign language.

As in the United States, you'll be able to count on camping-associated activities beyond pure tourism. Boat rentals are often part and parcel of a campground near water, should you want to go for a paddle, row, or outboard cruise. There's plenty of hiking to be had in the mountainous countries, and magnificent scenery that rivals our own Western Rockies.

Fishing is another sport you can count on, but the great majority of waters are under private control. Make sure you have both an appropriate license and an understanding with the owner before you wet a line.

Hunting is generally more problematical, primarily because of the private nature of lands and firearms restrictions. If you would like to hunt while in Europe, lay your plans and get firm commitments well in advance of your trip.

Costs involved when you camp in Europe are largely up to you. If you keep a very tight rein on your billfold and settle for minimum comforts, you can do your trip very cheaply. We can cite one family of four that lived on $40 a week (without gas costs). A more practical and comfortable estimate, though, would fall between $10 and $15 per day for two—and that includes gas, gifts, and an occasional bottle of whisky or wine.

208

Perhaps the best way to determine how much you might spend would be to cite some specifics.

• Round-trip air fare to Europe for one, economy class, runs around $300.

• Gasoline costs $.80 a gallon.

• Food prices are comparable to United States levels, with the exception of meats (particularly beef) which are sky-high. National dishes, or their components, are usually cheap—sauerkraut, weiners, and beer in Germany, bakery goods in the Scandinavian countries, for example.

• Campgrounds cost $.80 a night.

• You can rent a small car and camping gear for $150 a week.

DRIVING in all of Europe (except for Britain) is on the right side of the road. Those roads are, however, quite narrow. So narrow, in fact, that we recommend you rent or buy a foreign "bug" in lieu of shipping your Cadillac or Lincoln over. The "bugs" are also economical on gas, and at $.80 a gallon (with high-octane gas hard to find), that's no small comfort.

Excellent road maps are available for all countries, but aren't handed out for free. You'll discover that all of Europe's road signs are in pictures, not words, so once you learn what they mean, you'll understand them in any country you tour.

While it isn't required, it's not a bad idea to get an international driver's license, either in the United States before you leave, or upon arrival in Europe. What is mandatory for any driver is "international green card in-

209

surance" (liability) for your vehicle. You must be so covered before you climb behind the wheel, and covered during your entire stay in Europe. Green card insurance is available at virtually any port of entry, and costs $40 for one month, $250 for a year. Coverage includes liability, fire, and theft, and is worth $275,000. Extra collision insurance is available.

RECVEES, so familiar on the highways of home, aren't too good an idea in Europe. Truck campers use a lot of gas and are too big for the roads. Travel trailers need a large car for towing, and the size of the trailer is severely restricted in some countries. Norway, for example, requires a special permit for trailers wider than 7 feet, 2 inches. Switzerland bans them entirely on many mountain roads.

Then, too, there's the initial cost of shipping them over from the United States. This will run you between $350 and $1,000 round trip, depending on the size and bulk of the unit.

Rather than bringing your transportation to Europe, we think a far better solution is to buy it while you're there.

BUYING A CAR IN EUROPE works in several ways for the camper. Their initial price is lower than you'd find stateside (an economy-class Volkswagen costs around $1,550 at the factory; a four-door Volvo sedan, $2,500) and they can be shipped back to the United States as a used car, reducing the duty and excise tax you'll have to pay.

Then too, as we pointed out before, European cars are designed for European roads. And European mechanics know how to fix them if they need repair.

To buy a car in Europe, you can make all the arrange-

210

ments through a stateside dealer. Volvo will even take your old car in trade, and apply its price to the purchase price of your new car overseas. Give the dealers six to ten weeks to get things set up. When you're done with your camping trip, the European dealer will arrange to have your car shipped home for you. This costs between $300 and nothing. If you drop a Volvo off at a designated port, and pick it up in New York, Baltimore, Jacksonville, or Houston, Volvo will give it a free ride.

Before you commit yourself to purchasing a car in Europe, however, make sure that the salesman is telling you about *all* the charges involved. Sometimes there are separate bills in addition to the cost of the car alone, and they mount up to a tidy sum.

When tallying up how much it will cost in taxes to bring your car home, figure duty at 4½ per cent of its worth at the time, and excise taxes at 7 per cent. Don't forget that this will all be prorated against the mileage you've put on, so a well-used car immigrates pretty cheaply.

9 Trails
That Lead
from Camp

Modern technology coupled with ever-growing interest in the outdoors has resulted in machinery that can transport man into country that was once the exclusive domain of two- and four-footed animals. The machines are more reliable than a dog team, safer than a horse, and as rugged as any mountain man. They're here, they're what's happening, and most of all, they're fun.

Trail bikes function as a pleasant way to travel on the open road, then double as rugged machines that will get you into roadless countryside. They're a great way to reach top hunting and fishing, and a short cut to the pleasures of wilderness wandering.

Snowmobiles have opened up new horizons and a whole season for the camper—winter. Properly dressed and well equipped, a snowmobiler can whiz through the woodlands on a cold-weather sight-seeing trip, or turn an empty snow field into a winter carnival for himself and his family.

Dune buggies turn any stretch of sandy beach or desert into a superhighway. They'll go anywhere around sand you want them to: along a wave-packed ocean beach, right up to a down-East clambake, or up and down desert dunes of wind-blown sand.

Folding boats, boats you blow up, and canoes that weigh next to nothing make lakes and rivers that were once off-limits as accessible as your bathtub. What's more, rubber boats now can be paddled and rowed with precision and ease, and will even take a water-skiing-sized outboard.

And there's a machine that will do everything too. It will carry you and your family across sand, mud, water, snow, and over rugged, rocky country. It's called an ATV, and it's truly the sporty and sporting machine of the future.

Some campers cuss these machines as either making access to the outdoors "too easy" or as being somehow detrimental to the environment. Off-the-road vehicles, and the opportunities they provide, can be used properly or abused —we won't argue that. But in responsible hands, they're worth their weight (and cost) in excitement, enjoyment, and limitless outdoor adventure.

TRAIL BIKES

Trail bikes amount to light motorcycles, with a gearing system that gets plenty of go out of a small amount of horsepower. There are two basic types of trail bikes. One kind, characterized by brands like Tote Gote and Bonanza, are rather short, dumpy-looking things. They have tires that are small in circumference, but extremely wide in tread. They usually have a centrifugal clutch as opposed to a standard gearing system, and achieve a top speed of around 30 miles an hour.

The other trail bike design is characterized by the

213

CAMPING IN COMFORT

Japanese lightweights: Honda, Yamaha, Suzuki, and Kawasaki. They have large bicycle-like tires, a headlamp, and an over-all motorcycle look. They also have a two-speed gear range, allowing trail riders to gear way down for mountain work, then switch to road gearing when they get back to asphalt. On the older models, this switch was accomplished by a sprocket change. Now it's done with the flick of a dial on most machines. They have a top road speed of 50 mph.

Because of their dual-purpose nature and over-all good looks (you wouldn't be ashamed to drive one to the office), we feel the latter design is a better deal for the comfortable camper. There's also the matter of suspension. The motorcycle trail bikes have good suspension, and their large wheels afford a smooth ride. The small mountain machines sometimes don't have any suspension at all, and when they do, it's rough-and-tough.

SELECTING A TRAIL BIKE. Here are a few points to consider when you're buying a trail bike. If your machine incorporates them, you'll cut the chances for on-the-trail mechanical problems to a minimum, and still get maximum use from your bike on the open road.

• If you're buying new, make sure your machine incorporates an easy switch-over feature when you want to change your gear range. Wrestling with a greasy sprocket is a dirty, messy job. Men tolerate it, but women won't.

• Keep your engine in the neighborhood of 90 cc's (that means cubic centimeters and is a measurement of the area inside your engine that contains the explosion and does the work, hence, an indication of power). A larger engine

214

than that will make your bike weigh too much. A smaller engine won't have power to push you at highway speed.

• Keep the weight of the bike as low as possible—150 pounds is just about right. More weight than that and you'll have to fight a lot of gravity on rough trails. If you're planning on trail bikes for the whole family, make sure the bike is light enough to be lifted by whoever will be riding it.

• Make sure the bike has good suspension. Bounce up and down on the seat to check for good cushioning.

• The lowest part of the bike, under the engine, should be a flat surface, preferably protected by an easy-to-remove skid plate. If any parts are exposed at this point, they're sure to get banged up on rough trails.

• Your electrical system—battery, wiring, and lights— should be up high. So should your source of air (breather) for your carburetor. This is to prevent short outs and flood outs when you ford a stream.

• You're wiser to keep "extras" to a minimum. Things like electric-start motors add extra weight and cost. Rear-view mirrors are bound to get torn loose after a few trips into rough country.

• Check the exhaust system very carefully. It should be situated in such a way that it can't touch your leg if you spill. The motor should also be fully muffled. It's not only easier on your ears—straight pipes are a tremendous fire hazard.

RIDING A TRAIL BIKE on the open road requires very little savvy. Once you learn to shift gears, it's much like a bicycle except you go a lot faster with a lot less work. Once

215

you get off the road and into back country, however, there are a few tricks to the trade. The first is in the clothing you wear.

Be prepared for slapping brush and abrasive rocks by wearing high-top boots and heavy pants. Gloves aren't a bad idea either, and a crash helmet is advisable.

Once you're on the trail, you'll find getting around logs requires the most work. If they're low to the ground—say a foot or so—get off your bike and "walk" it over. Hold onto the handlebars, point your front wheel where you want it to go, and give your machine a little gas. It should climb up and over all by itself. If the log is too high for this operation, you'll have to get some help lifting it over the top or sliding it underneath. That's one of the many reasons for lightness in a trail bike. It's also a good idea to turn off your engine whenever both wheels will be off the ground at the same time.

Fording streams is wet, but fun. First, of course, make sure the water isn't deeper than you. Generally, a well-made bike will go in 2 to 2½ feet of water. Deeper than that and it drowns.

Approach the stream in low or second gear. Don't go too fast or you'll get soaked from the spray and have trouble controlling. If the stream is paved with big, slippery rocks, you're going to have to do some steadying with your feet as you cross.

You're wise to get off and walk your bike over extremely rocky terrain. It isn't too hard on the bike, but it will be on the seat of your pants if you try to stay in the saddle.

The same advice goes for extremely steep hills. The bike

will have enough power to make it, but chances are you won't have the exquisite balance needed and will up-end.

In both operations, put your machine in low gear, give it a little gas, and walk at its side. It will help pull you along as you steady it. Don't give it too much gas—it might take off without you.

Conservationists have two legitimate complaints about the trail-bike rider, and they amount to something of a lesson in courtesy and good outdoor sense to prospective bikers.

The first complaint is that trail bikes startle horses. They certainly do. I was once on my horse—a pretty gentle, sensible animal, used to all manner of distractions—when a poorly muffled trail bike passed us by. I could feel the creature trembling under my thighs. Given the right combination—say a packstring of dudes and a skittish horse or two—a trail bike in unthinking hands could spell havoc and very possibly tragedy. So, when you see horses on the trail, either give them a wide berth (at least a hundred yards), or pull well off to the side of the trail and turn off your engine until they pass you by.

The second complaint is more often cited than the first, and is just as valid. Trail bikes, because they're on wheels, leave an arrow-straight track when they go through soft earth. Unlike the pockmarks of human or animal footprints, these tracks are an open invitation for water to drain and for soil to erode. The ultimate result of this kind of careless biking is an ugly gully—an open sore in the side of the earth.

To avoid being responsible for this kind of ecological

damage, make it a rule (1) not to use your bike when it's muddy (they're hellish things to handle in mud anyway) and (2) never to go straight up the side of a hill unless there's a permanent trail there. Either climb the hill by traversing it, or hop off your bike and walk it up.

TRANSPORTING THE BIKE to wherever you want to use it on your camping itinerary presents no real problem.

A trail bike will easily fit in the back of a pickup camper or travel trailer. Just make sure you have it lashed down well.

Trail-bike brackets can be bought at cycle shops. They fit on your back or front bumper (or both) and carry your machine by holding the wheels in slots.

There's also a rig that trailers your bike without a trailer. The bike's front wheel lifts up off the ground and fits into a rear-bumper bracket. The rear wheel just rolls along as you do.

And here's something for the camper with limited space —say a touring houseboater who wants to bring some shoreside transportation along with him. Several manufacturers boast of take-down models: trail bikes with handle bars that fold down, foot pegs and pedals that fold up and out of the way for easy storage. We've seen one bike that breaks down into two suitcase-sized packages—and they give you the suitcases when you buy the bike!

SNOWMOBILES

Snowmobiles are thought by some to be a brand-new invention. Actually, machines that use the snowmobile principle have been around since the 1930's. What is new about them, however, is that they're much smaller, more compact, and a lot less expensive than they used to be.

Snowmobiles get their mobility via two things: weight displacement and a moving track. Imagine a pair of skis or snowshoes—the time-tested way for travel over snow. They support a man because they distribute his weight over a large area of snow, and prevent him from sinking in. A snowmobile stays on top for the same reason; there's a large, flat surface area underneath so the machine floats on top of snow and doesn't bog down.

Their go is supplied by way of a continuous belt, like the track on a tank or bulldozer. A motor drives the belt, and the belt moves the machine.

• Before you buy a snowmachine, you'll want to decide between two alternatives: whether to purchase one big machine for the whole family, or buy one small machine for each rider. This sounds a bit oversimplified, but it isn't. Large, powerful machines can pull a bunch of skiers, or a toboggan full of family behind them. But they're expensive—around $1,500. Small machines have plenty of go with one aboard, lug a little with two, and can't pull a very big load of skiers. But they can be had as cheaply as $700.

Before you decide one way or the other, let's take a further look at what each kind of machine offers.

Large models usually boast of quite a bit of horsepower —30 to 40 hp isn't unusual. They also frequently have twin tracks—two turning belts, side-by-side, for greater stability and "go" with a heavy load. Because they're so large and heavy, options such as electric starting and re-

219

verse gear are wise, though costly, inclusions in your purchase. If your snowmobiling tastes lean toward family outings, or if your children are too young to drive a small snowmobile themselves, the big models are probably the best bet for you. You can load a picnic lunch and the people who are going to eat it in a ski-trailer, snug a passenger up behind you on the machine, and be off for a day in a wintry wonderland.

These big machines are also the most dependable in that they can handle virtually any snow condition that might develop. So they're best too if you're the hardy kind of outdoorsman who will be traveling at 20 degrees below, as well as in the wet, mushy snow of spring.

Small machines have horsepower ranging from 15 to 30. They usually have a single track, making them more maneuverable than the big ones, but they're less stable on turns and in hilly terrain. They're reasonably light too, and can be manhandled out of a tough spot, so you'll save some money by not needing reverse gear. Their motors are small enough to start by hand too, so there's another saving.

Small snowmobiles are most satisfactory for the family with growing youngsters, old enough to take a machine of their own. They're exciting fun on one-man-to-a-machine trail rides, when everyone cuts trails in the sparkling snow, doing his own thing. Small snowmobiles can also be family snowmobiles if you limit your family activity to ideal snow conditions. More about that later.

Once you decide on the size and price of the machine that suits your purposes best, performance should be the next consideration. It's rather tough to tell what kind of product you'll be getting in a shiny showroom, but here are a few features that should help to narrow your choice down.

• Horsepower means money—the more you get, the more you pay. If you'll be snowmobiling in the flatlands of Michigan or Minnesota, and don't plan to enter any races, you won't need a monster of an engine to get you around. Conversely, if you'll be traveling the rugged mountains of Montana or Wyoming, you're going to need power for long, hard pulls.

• Steering is achieved by skis on the front of your snow-mobile. Two steering skis are far superior to one in terms of control, stability, and flotation.

• Your seat is an extremely essential bit of equipment and its quality determines if you'll be eating off the mantelpiece that night. Get a very soft, comfortable one.

• The track or tracks that make your machine go have ripples in them for gripping. They can be either pure rubber or rubber topped with steel. Steel tracks are best for packed, crusted, or wet snow, but leave a little to be desired in powder snow. Rubber tracks don't cut and grip as well as steel, but perform well in powder. Choose according to the conditions that will be prevalent in your area.

• Tracks occasionally need attention. They have to be adjusted for correct fit and tension. Make sure the adjustments on your prospective machine are placed so you can get the job done without going through a major overhaul.

• Mufflers, and demanding their installation on our machines, are a personal must for us. Neither of us can stand the incessant rap-rap-rap of an unmuffled machine. It gives us a headache and is aesthetically out of place in a world of quiet white.

221

CAMPING IN COMFORT

RIDING THE SNOWMACHINE requires a little touch, so you're wise to start out slowly until you get the feel of the thing. And by the way, you should use the buddy system if you're venturing into the back country. Always have a companion and a second snowmobile along for help in case of trouble.

The first time on a snowmobile will be easiest on you and it if you solo; make it a match between man and machine that doesn't include other passengers or trailing sleds. When you give a snowmobile the gas (usually done by way of a lever or a twist handle), it moves forward. There's no shifting, thanks to a gadget called a centrifugal clutch. When you release the gas, it stops. That's simple enough, and that's really all there is to it—so long as you drive in a straight line over a flat surface.

When you get into a turning situation, however, you've got to do a little work. You've got to lean to the inside of the curve—the faster the speed and sharper the turn, the greater the lean. It's much like riding a bicycle, except a bike leans with you naturally. A snowmachine doesn't lean at all.

When approaching a dip—a gully or snow-covered stream —get up off the seat and let your legs absorb the shock. If you don't, at the very least you will bang the seat really hard, and at the worst, will get bucked off into a snowbank.

Don't tackle too great a hill until you know your machine well. And remember that the machine will climb a steeper grade than it can turn around on. If you try to turn around halfway up too steep an incline, you'll either turn over, slide down sideways, or bury your machine out of sight.

When going up any hill, don't stop until you reach the

top. You've got momentum going for you, and if you don't use it to your advantage, chances are you'll have to go back down and start all over again. This is particularly true when you're dragging a sled or skier.

No matter how good you and your machine are, there will be times when you'll bog down—when your track will dig itself down in the snow and your machine will sink. When you find you can't make any headway, don't try it any more—things will just get worse. Try to back out gracefully (if you have a reverse gear; alternatively, dismount and shove.) If that's impossible, get a friend to pull you out with a rope.

If there's no friend and you're really stuck, all you've got left to do is dig. Dig all the snow from around your machine, and make a gradually sloping ramp that will lead you out of the hole. Pack it down well with your feet for added support. You also might try stuffing some branches under your machine for added traction. With a little shoving, heaving, huffing, and puffing, you should climb right out.

SNOW CONDITIONS. To the average American, snow was just plain snow until fifteen years ago. Then skiing began to catch on, and like the Eskimo, winter sportsmen learned there's a tremendous variety in the consistency and quality of snow.

There are powder snow, pack snow, corn snow, crusty snow, dry snow, wet snow—almost as many names as breakfast cereals. The snowmobiler, however, needs to concern himself with only three basic kinds of white stuff. Understanding the conditions that bring these snows about, plus how they will affect your machine performance, will help you decide what you can and can't do on a particular outing.

Dry snow occurs when fresh snow falls and the temperature doesn't get above freezing. Most of our northernmost states have dry snow throughout the winter, since their temperatures seldom get above 32 degrees. Dry snow won't make good snowballs, and is soft to the touch.

Snowmobiles really move out in dry snow, but they can't carry much weight without bogging down. The driver has excellent control of the vehicle too, so it's a good time to learn the ropes. Don't forget that dry snow means biting-cold temperatures, so dress warmly.

Crusted snow happens because the snow melts a bit in the heat of the sun, then refreezes when the temperature drops. The surface of the snow will have a sugary crust, and it will resist the pressure of a hand.

This kind of snow means you can count on great latitude with your machine. You're not likely to bog down, so you can carry an extra passenger along with you. The crust also offers little slide-resistance, so you can probably pull a skier or a sled to boot, or hit some very fast speeds if you're alone.

Crusted snow doesn't lend itself well to traction or control though. You might slide backwards trying to climb a hill, and will probably do some side-slipping when you come into a fast turn.

Wet snow is the worst stuff for any kind of winter sports except building snowmen and snowballing. It puts up quite a bit of slide-resistance, and has a supportive consistency that's worse than powder. Snowmobiling is popular in wet

224

snow though, because it invariably means warm sunshine and spring-like temperatures.

Don't overload if you're traveling over wet snow, and don't try to pull too big a load. If there are packed trails where you're going, stay on them, and when you're going uphill, maintain your momentum.

If you start bogging down a lot, turn off your engine and check your undercarriage. Chances are the snow has packed in under there and doubled your weight. Clean it out with the motor *off*. If you still have trouble, try waxing your front skis, or any sliding surfaces you might be dragging behind you. Use wet-snow ski wax (red in color), and rub it on in a squiggly pattern.

Perhaps one more kind of snow deserves discussion: not enough.

When there's only a light cover on the ground, or the spotty snowbanks of a spring thaw, stay off your machine. The same goes for fording unfrozen streams and running your machine across dry roads. Sometimes it's a necessity, but remember that every time you hit a rock or bare ground, you're wearing essential parts, and those parts aren't cheap to replace.

CLOTHING is extremely important to the snowmobiler and his family. You're operating in cold conditions to begin with, and when you're under way, the wind/chill factor makes it a lot colder than the thermometer reads.

A whole line of specially designed garments has sprung up around the current snowmobile craze, and these are far superior to garments you might scrounge out of the attic.

CAMPING IN COMFORT

Generally, the warmest clothes are of the "flight suit" design—bottoms and tops are all one unit that you step into and zip up. Extremities are the most susceptible to frostbite, so thick snowmobiler's bootees and mittens are the order of the day. A hat covered by a hood is great protection for your head and ears, and when it's really cold, a face mask is practically mandatory.

Goggles are a good move all the way around. They protect your eyes from the brutal glare of sun off snow, keep them from tearing in the cold, and protect them from the dangers of unseen branches.

TRANSPORTING the snowmobile is largely a matter of trailering. Most manufacturers turn out trailers that will hold two of their machines. One of the slickest ideas we've seen in a long time was a gadget we ran into at a recent snowmobilers' convention: a trailer that converted into a sled.

ANIMALS. One of the many joys of snowmobiling is the access it provides to wintering wildlife. But that advantage is too often abused and becomes a singular discredit to the sport.

Animals on their winter range are in a weakened state. Reduced food supplies, plus the sheer work of bucking snow and keeping warm, hold their strength and health at a low ebb. When they see a snowmobile, they of course become frightened. If it comes too close, they run and use up still more valuable energy. Many deer, elk, moose, and even rabbits, never live to see the spring because of a snowmobiler's thoughtlessness.

When you see animals on your winter outings, give them a wide berth. Go out of your way to avoid spooking them.

That little gesture on your part could well mean the gift of life to them.

DUNE BUGGIES

Dune buggies are a bit more difficult to define than trail bikes or snowmobiles. They can be anything from an old jalopy with a locked rear end to a balloon-tired four-wheel-drive truck. The most recent additions to the family are the sleek new fiberglass bodies bolted on Volkswagen frames that are being turned out by the thousands on both coasts, and go by a hundred trade names.

But even with such vast differences in styles and origin, there are features common to any vehicle that wants to be known as a "dune buggy."

Tires are the key to a successful sand machine. Sand is soft, loose-consistency stuff, and in order to get where you want to go, you have to "float" over it, much in the way that a snowmobile stays on top of snow. To stay up there, you need great, wide, balloon-like tires. The heavier the vehicle, the wider the tire. Cut-down cars, like the little two-seater fiberglass buggies, can get by with standard road tires in the 8.00 range. Larger vehicles that carry more weight need specially designed tires.

These tires are often too wide to fit correctly on a conventional rim, so to make them bulge out and increase the surface contact between sand and rubber, "split rims" are often employed. These amount to a wheel rim cut with an acetylene torch into two halves. A strip of steel is welded in the cut, and the rim is wider.

Another operation common to dune buggies is a locked

rear end. Factory-produced autos have a thing called a slip differential—a rear axle setup that allows power to be thrown to only one wheel at a time. By locking the rear end, you get power thrown to both wheels at once, doubled traction and go-power. This locked-rear-end effect can be achieved by a $10 welding job, but largely limits your buggy to off-the-road driving. A locked rear end on pavement causes excessive tire wear.

You can get the same effect by buying your sand vehicle equipped with a non-slip differential, or by installing one yourself. Costs are a little steeper here—about $150.

Roll bars are an important safety measure as it's surprisingly easy to flip or roll over on sand. Stout, steel bars should be welded to the frame and reach well above the passenger's head. That way, if you do flip, the weight of the vehicle rests on the roll bars and not on you. Because of that same tendency to flip, and a generally jouncy, bouncy ride, seat belts and crash helmets are absolutely necessary.

One other feature to look for or install yourself seems a bit ridiculous in a rough-and-tumble vehicle: hubcaps. But there's a reason. Sand permeates everything and you want to keep it out of your wheel hubs. Sand is extremely abrasive, and will grind away at bearings, spindles, and most commonly, brake drums, until there's nothing left. Hubcaps at least cut that wear to a minimum.

You might remember that if you're thinking about buying a secondhand machine, put wheel hubs at the top of your list when you're inspecting for wear.

How much should you expect to pay? Some years ago, I put together a great little dune buggy from junked parts for under $150. If you're looking for class, good looks, and a second car to knock around town in, those fiberglass bodies on Volkswagen frames sell in the neighborhood of $1,600.

TRANSPORTING THE BUGGY. If you don't want to drive, the buggy can be transported via trailer, but a trailer large and strong enough to carry the weight of a car can be pretty expensive. We think the best way by far is the tow-bar arrangement.

A hinged, stout tow bar is bolted or welded (welding is far superior and safer) to the front bumper of your buggy. It, in turn, snugs up to a ball hitch on your family car's rear bumper. When you go down the road, your buggy follows like a trailer, and also serves as a place to stow extra gear. When using the buggy, the tow bar can be removed, or swung up out of the way.

DRIVING THE BUGGY. (See also "Off-the-road driving," Chapter 2.) Mud, snow, and sand seem like pretty diverse bedfellows, but at least in terms of driving they all have one thing in common. In order to get around on wheels, you've got to keep up your momentum. Get moving and keep moving. If you have to stop, try to do it on a downgrade.

Desert driving in a dune buggy virtually always means dry sand. In this stuff, it pays to stay in the tracks somebody else made. The sand there is at least a little packed, and you avoid the resistance put up by the sand you'll be pushing out of your way when you make your own track.

Staying in the tracks has another thing going for it too—you'll be helping to preserve the environment. Desert ecology is extremely fragile. It takes ten years for a sprig of brush to grow, and only a second to kill it. It's been almost thirty years since World War II, but the tracks practicing tanks left are still very much in evidence on our Southwestern deserts. If everyone who owned a dune buggy decided to "make his own track," we feel safe in saying our deserts would be ripped clean of half their vegetation in ten years.

Driving on ocean beaches is a bit easier and more predictable than on deserts for one reason: there's plenty of water. When sand gets wet, it packs and gets hard. It will support your tires much more efficiently than when dry. When driving on ocean beach, get down close to the water. You'll find a smooth, hard-packed superhighway there. But a word of warning—don't get too close to the water. Changing tides and currents cause "slush pots," pockets of sand and water trapped behind low sand bars, and barely perceptible to even a trained eye. If you get into a slush pot, nothing short of a two-speed winch will pull you out. Because they're usually located close to the low-tide mark, you won't have much time to find that winch either.

Your best bet is to travel just below the highest point reached by the lapping waves of the last high tide. The sand there will be a bit softer than right down next to the pounding surf, but your chances of running into a slush pot are nil. If, because of a sand shelf or high dunes, you have to travel close to the water, watch out for little dips and depressions in an otherwise flat beach. They're about the only indication of a possible slush pot ahead.

Within reason, the entire beach is yours when you own a buggy. You can scout for striped bass in the surf, find a spot where the waves are breaking just right for exciting surfboarding, or just hole up in a secluded spot and have an old-fashioned beach party and clambake. But stick to the beach and stay off the dunes. Dunes are often the only protection seacoast dwellers have between a raging, stormy sea and calm inland waters.

Salt grass, dune grass, and beach plum bushes are every bit as delicate as a desert plant, and they're what's holding the dunes in place. Drive across them once or twice and, more likely than not, you'll open a cut that will let the sea in on the first stormy day.

BOATS BEYOND CAMP

Boats big enough to camp in or with were the subject of the chapter on "Boat Camping," so if you're interested in bringing a large boat with you on your camping trip, check there.

There are, however, a whole new breed of boats being turned out, particularly well suited to casual use and easy, space-saving transport. They're ideal as a fishing platform for a shoreside camp, and double as a boat for the kids to paddle and play in on the shores of a lonely lake. They're not "toys" however. Each of them is responsive to a paddle and seaworthy. Some of them can even be used with an outboard. They're well designed and well constructed for years of hard use, and that, plus their compactness, is good news indeed.

BLOW-UP BOATS once amounted to one thing: a rubber raft. These craft were unresponsive to oars, motors, and aside from specialized use on white-water rivers, had little practical application in a camping situation.

231

Now, however, boats you blow up take a shape far more practical than an elongated washtub. Some of them look like kayaks, some like canoes, and some look (and are) like outboard runabouts.

When choosing a blow-up boat, look for two things: rubberized canvas and rigidity.

Rubberized canvas is strong and puncture resistant. While you must take reasonable care when around sharp snags and rocks, it does take quite a punch to put a hole through the material. Stay clear of plastic material without a cloth backing. These things *are* toys.

Rigidity means responsive handling. When you flick a paddle or start an outboard, a rigid boat will move out. This rigidity is usually achieved either by a network of air-filled tubing or by solid ribs or floors (usually aluminum tubing for the ribs, or plywood sheeting for the floor).

A good test of rigidity is to blow your boat up, then pick it up in the middle. If it droops and bends, getting it to respond properly will be like paddling in an inner tube with short arms. If it holds its shape well, you can assume it will handle accordingly.

Blow-up boats range in size from a 6-foot kayak to a 16-foot runabout. The runabout will take up to a 30-horse engine, and will even tow a water skier! Prices run roughly from $80 to $1,000. Avon, a European company, makes some of the better blow-ups.

FOLDING BOATS are other spacesavers, and because of their rigidity, handle even better than the best blow-up boat. They're usually of the kayak design, boast of lengths of up to 18 feet, and cost from $200 to $600.

232

The larger boats fold up into several packages. Each section is assembled, then bolted together to form the finished hull. Although they're heavier than blow-up boats, and just as vulnerable to damage, they have one pleasant advantage in terms of diversity: they can be rigged with a sail.

ULTRALIGHT CANOES are probably the best choice in small boats for the avid fisherman and hunter. Although they're of rigid construction and must be car-topped, their light weight (30 to 50 pounds) means you can carry them any-place—even on top of a light camper shell.

Light weight isn't their only asset. They're very short by canoe standards—12 to 15 feet—and can handle both a small outboard and a payload of around 800 pounds.

Sportspal makes the lightest, an aluminum canoe that weighs a scant 29½ pounds. Orvis makes a similar product from fiberglass that's slightly heavier. Prices on these ultra-lights start at around $300 and go up from there.

ATV's

All Terrain Vehicles (ATV's) are machines that truly make reality out of a sportsman's fondest dream. Their name says it all. They'll roll over rugged hills that would stop a trail bike, wallow through mud that would stop anything else, scoot over snow, and even float on water with a forward speed of 2 to 4 knots.

They achieve this by incorporating several features, the most important of which is the Terra Tire. The Terra Tire is a great balloony tire with extremely low pressure (1½ to

233

2 pounds). Like balloon tires on a dune buggy and the track of a snowmobile, these tires distribute the weight of the vehicle over a large area so it "floats" across unstable surfaces. Flotation is also increased because most of these machines boast of more than four tires—six, eight, even ten. All those wheels have power on them too. They all turn, churn, and achieve tremendous traction.

In the water, watertight bodies, plus the floatability of air-filled tires, keep you well above the waves. The tread of the turning tires acts like a paddle wheel to propel you forward. Some models even incorporate a mount for an outboard or a propeller, for greater speed.

Right now there are over fifty brands of ATV's on the market, and the trend is just getting under way. There will probably be at least another fifty climbing on the band wagon in the next decade. So where do you begin to look for the model that suits you best?

By first weeding out those that don't adequately incorporate the "all-terrain" features you're buying your machine for. Any ATV, if it's going to live up to its name, should perform at least nominally in sand, mud, water, and hilly terrain. Not all of them do.

Water seems to be their biggest Achilles' heel. Many brands will float and chug through the water, but their low freeboard and instability make them dangerous. You can't operate them in a chop or swift river current without danger of swamping.

Snow performance is another thing to consider. Many of these machines will only navigate hardpack. This limitation, of course, would be undesirable if you lived in northern

234

Minnesota, but it wouldn't make too much difference to a resident of Florida.

After you've narrowed your choice to the brands that do the job you want them to, here are a few other considerations.

The more wheels the ATV has, the better performance you can expect. This, of course, jacks the price up too.

An articulated body, one that's hinged so it can twist to meet the contours of the earth, achieves the most traction.

Because of the beating your machine is bound to take, make sure the body is reinforced at stress points. Metal bodies don't seem to hold up as well as well-constructed fiberglass or ABS plastic, especially if you're using your machine in a wet or ocean climate.

The best goers in mud or snow are those ATV's that are set up for tracks (like a bulldozer). Most pleasant here are tracks that can be added directly over the Terra Tire, rather than permanent tracks that take long hours to install.

Many manufacturers tout top speeds in excess of 30 mph as one of their selling points. You pay extra for such high speeds, and they're of little use. The kind of country you're buying your machine for just doesn't lend itself to speeds beyond a crawl, and you're obviously not going to cruise the highways in an ATV. After all, if you're outdoorsing on smooth, high-speed ground, why not do it in real comfort and buy an air-conditioned Cadillac?

One other point to look for in your machine is load capacity. Many of the ATV's have seating for only two, plus a minimal amount of room for gear. This is something of a disadvantage, both for the family man and the avid outdoorsman. Generally, seating for four means two people can carry enough gear for a week of reasonably comfortable camping.

While it's quite true that you can't expect all these features in an economy-line vehicle, several middle-of-the-roaders we've seen do incorporate them. Prices on this kind of unit run from $1,200 to $2,000. If you want to spend more, the big units designed for resorts and guides offer maximum comfort, room, and mobility. Prices on them start at $4,000 and go up. If you want to get your feet wet on a small, inexpensive model first, figure on an $800 cash outlay.

ATV's have one other important feature. Because of their huge tires, they do little if any damage to soil and hillsides, so even from a conservation standpoint, ATV's are shaping up as the sportsman's friend of the future.

236

10 Reading, Writing, Recreation, and Recipes

Camping is, by its very nature, an outdoor pastime, but before you leave on any trip or set that first tent stake, you'd be wise to get some indoor exercise under your belt by reading, writing, and some general research.

The following is a collection of odds and ends that will help to make your trip more pleasant and simplify your planning procedure. It includes things as diversified as camp recipes and camping clubs, Fineagle's Laws of Camping, addresses of state recreation agencies, and a list of other books you might like to glance through on cold winter nights while you wait for spring.

It's all information that we've found very useful, and we're sure it will prove the same to you.

FINEAGLE'S LAWS OF CAMPING

Francis X. Fineagle (1929–   ) is a man with whom we've shared and enjoyed many a campfire. His wit, perception, and ability never cease to amaze us, and his advice has been proven valid by the test of time.

237

CAMPING IN COMFORT

Unfortunately, Francis has never written down or otherwise recorded his observations on camping lore. We've tried to keep track of them, but because of unavailability of paper and pencil at appropriate times, our accumulation of data is partial at best. Still, even the scant information we've been able to assemble amounts to invaluable help and advice. We hope, through Francis's help, to eventually put together a complete set of laws and postulates, for we know they'll prove to be of immeasurable aid to campers of all persuasions.

On Buying Camping Equipment

The desire and justification for new camping equipment will always exceed the money available for its purchase.

- (A) Those items claimed to be the most needed will always turn out to be the least useful.
- (B) The least useful items will invariably have the most moving parts (see "On Things Mechanical").
  - (1) Camping gear with moving parts has an irresistible attraction for male campers, not unlike the lure of flame to moth.

On Things Mechanical

If something can break down, it will.

- (A) The chances for a mechanical breakdown are directly proportional to that object's number of moving parts.
- (B) Careful planning to rectify any problems caused by a mechanical breakdown insures a long life for that machine (e.g., when you bring an auxiliary outboard motor because your old standby has been acting

strangely, the old machine will perform as well as the day you bought it).

(1) The day you don't bring a replacement, the old outboard will self-destruct.

When you fail to grasp how or why a machine works, it is bound to break down with predictable regularity.

(A) The longer the time spent trying to fix it, the greater the chance it will never work again.

(1) If you play with something long enough, it will break.

(2) There will always be someone to play with it.

(B) If, by long chance, the repair job is successful, you won't be able to remember what it was you did right.

ON PACKING

The more useful the item, the more likely you are to forget it. Thyme will be remembered and packed long before salt, a can opener will turn up missing when you have two pairs of salad tongs, and you'll remember a dash of bitters makes a good Manhattan, but forget ice.

(A) You won't notice they're missing until the moment you need them most.

(B) As soon as you buy a replacement, you'll discover you had the missing item all along.

No matter how carefully you pack, whatever you need first will be at the bottom of the heaviest equipment you own.

(A) You'll swear it was lost while packing and blame somebody else.

239

(B) When you find it, you'll make some comment about poor organization and blame somebody else.

(C) You'll find it in your pocket, purse, or under the front seat of the car.

On Choosing Campsites

The site you select will be adjudged the best available. At the moment you complete setting up your camp. . .

(A) The best site in the campground will be vacated.

(B) Junior will find a better site just over the hill.

(C) Someone will tell you camping isn't permitted on the spot you chose, and point to a prominent sign you didn't see.

On Campfires

The greater the need for a campfire, the harder it will be to start.

(A) Campfires will start themselves on days when you'd like to eat a cold salad.

(B) Cool, rainy mornings and dark, damp nights require a copy of the Sunday *New York Times* and three books of matches before a flame will catch.

   (1) Even then, you have a 50/50 chance.

(C) The desire for a campfire increases as the wood supply dwindles.

No matter where you locate your campfire, you'll be directly in the path of smoke.

(A) When you move, so will the smoke.

   (1) It will be attracted to the greatest number of people it can reach.

(B) Once you locate so far from the fire that you can

no longer feel its warmth or see by its light, the smoke will rise straight in the air.

Cooking over a campfire will result in one of three things: a burned main course, a burned index finger, or at least one pot tipping over and putting out the fire.

(A) Sometimes all three will happen.

   (1) The chances for all three happening increase proportionally to the intricacy of your cooking supports.

   (2) Green willows cradled in forked sticks for a cooking support amount to a sure thing.

(B) The odds against a campfire chef decrease as experience increases.

Campfires will always be harder to put out than they were to start.

(A) The tenacity with which they cling to kindling temperature will be determined by your distance from a supply of water. The farther you are, the more water you'll need to put them dead out.

(B) Ten minutes previous to your planned dousing, someone will add a fresh supply of fueling wood.

CAMP RECIPES

With a little work and imagination, no meal is beyond the camp chef. You can roast a stuffed turkey in a Dutch oven, prepare prime ribs of beef on a spit, and even cook delicate sauces and desserts over coals as well as you can on a kitchen range.

Although we've done all these things, we can't honestly

241

say they're everyday camp meals. Certain dishes just seem to lend themselves to outdoor cooking and living in terms of taste, ease of preparation, and the cooking and eating equipment required.

So here's a basic sampling of those recipes we've learned to lean on when we're living outdoors. Some of them are delightfully simple, like a BLT Sandwich and Sheepherder's Stew. Consider a meal like that after a hard day's hike or a long day's drive when all you've got on your mind is food and some sacktime. Because they're well suited to quickie camping, we've marked these ultra-simple recipes with a "Q."

Many of the recipes require a little time to prepare. Those that go well with a campfire are marked "T" for tent camping. Those that are easiest to prepare over a kitchen range are marked "A" for auto or recvee campers. These dishes, like barbecued roasts and chicken, and the New England Clambake, are just the ticket for a main-course meal and a full family, including, perhaps, those friendly people you just met from the next campsite.

When cooking up your camp meals, try to prepare and serve them so there's little work left after dinner; use throwaway foil instead of roasting pans, cook canned goods in the open can, and eat and drink from paper plates and cups. Think in terms of one-dish meals too—stews and meat/vegetable combinations that can all go into one quick-to-clean-up pot.

It also pays to incorporate some foresight into your cooking plans. When you have fried potatoes for supper, make extra so you can serve them with bacon and eggs for breakfast. And make lots of bacon too. Put with lettuce and

242

tomato between two slices of bread, it makes a great on-the-road sandwich.

And don't forget that all these recipes can be cooked at home too. Right in your kitchen or over a patio barbecue grill. It's a sure bet that once you try them, you'll want to eat and enjoy them again and again, for you'll find they bring memories of your camp outs right to your doorstep.

(Q) Stick-to-the-Ribs Oatmeal

This is a high-energy, one-pot, hurry-up breakfast that will satisfy hungry campers even though they don't have their customary bacon and eggs.

> 2 cups instant oatmeal
> ½ cup raisins or chopped dried fruit
> ½ cup nuts, crushed
> Milk or cream, and sugar to serve with the oatmeal

Cook oatmeal according to package instructions, adding fruit and nuts as soon as the oatmeal has absorbed the water you added. Serve with milk or cream, and sugar.

(Q, T, or A) Spicy Burger on a Bun

This meal is an old-time favorite with picnickers and barbe-cuers. If a quickie meal is on your mind, serve your burgers with potato chips and cold baked beans.

Should you be tenting, with some time and a warm campfire at your side, try Mickey's Potatoes and roast corn on the cob as a side dish.

243

CAMPING IN COMFORT

For truly fast preparation, a friend of ours makes up the spiced patties at home, then freezes them in individual foil packages. All she has to do is slide them onto griddle or grate, wait ten minutes, and her meal is ready.

1½ pounds ground beef
¼ cup chopped green pepper
¼ cup pimiento
¼ cup minced onions
2¼ teaspoons margarine or butter
   Salt and pepper to taste
6–8 hamburger buns
   Catsup
   Relish

Sauté green peppers, onion, and pimiento in margarine or butter. Mix well with the ground beef, salt, and pepper. Form into 6 to 8 patties. Cook in a frying pan or over coals until brown on both sides. This should take from 5 to 10 minutes on each side. Split buns in half and toast them. Serve hamburgers on the buns with catsup and relish. Serves 4 to 6.

(T) Sheepherder's Stew

If you need to prepare a hearty campfire meal in a hurry, this is the recipe for you.

Prepare the following for each person who will be eating:

½ pound diced meat (substitute hamburger or other ground meat)
1 small carrot cut in thin slices
1 small potato cut in thin slices
½ teaspoon dried minced onion
1 square foot heavy aluminum foil
1 bouillon cube dissolved in ½ cup hot water
   Salt and pepper to taste

Combine meat, carrot, potato, and onion in center of square of foil and sprinkle with seasonings. Pour bouillon broth over mixture, fold foil around it, seal loosely, leaving some space for steam expansion, and bury package in coals. Cook 20 to 30 minutes in hot coals. Pour juices into cup and drink as a hot broth; eat stew directly out of foil package. The broth can be thickened with flour and used as a gravy.

(T) Doughboys

Here is a recipe that's good for a quick dessert and will keep the children busy while you do the dishes.

> 1 cup Bisquick mix
> ¼ cup milk
> 2–4 tablespoons jelly

Place Bisquick mix in bowl, add milk, and stir. (Should make a soft dough.) Divide the dough into a portion for each eater and roll each portion between floured hands onto a smooth stick. Pinch one end of dough tight to hold it on the stick. Have the children cook the dough over coals, turning it frequently until lightly browned and cooked through. Remove from stick and pour jelly into the hole that's left.

(T) Mickey's Potatoes

Baked potatoes are admittedly a simple dish, but here's a way to make them cook twice as fast without burning their delicious skins.

Pierce each potato to be served on two sides with the tines of a fork. Nest them in individual squares of heavy-duty aluminum foil. Add one teaspoon of water. Wrap, seal, and bury the potatoes in the coals of your cooking fire. It should take from 30 to 40 minutes for a large potato to bake. They're done when you can pierce them to the center, then easily remove the knife blade or fork.

Camping and fishing go together like ham and eggs, but too many anglers think the fun's over once their quarry is caught. Fish are one of the best-tasting and most nutritious foods we can eat, and what's more, their flesh can be converted into a hundred unusual meals.

Below are two of our favorite fish recipes for camp outs. They work well on virtually any species of fish, fresh water or salt. Although you'll note that they're largely tied to trout, this is purely a matter of personal preference and condition. Trout are one of the most common fish in our Rocky Mountain West, and are one of our favorites on the table.

(T or A) Crackling Fried Trout

8 small trout, 5–7 inches long
1 egg, beaten
½ cup cracker crumbs
  Cooking oil for deep frying
  Salt and pepper

Clean the trout, leaving heads and tails intact. Dip in beaten egg, then cracker crumbs. (Don't use trout larger than 7 inches.) Heat oil to 375° F. and add trout—in a basket if you have one. Cook until the tail is as crisp as a potato chip. (If the fish are soft and moist inside, you haven't cooked them long enough.) Dry off the oil on absorbent paper towels, sprinkle with salt and pepper to taste, and eat. Bones and all, if you like.

(T or A) Burgundy Baked Trout

2½-pound trout, dressed
⅛ pound butter or margarine
1 cup dry red wine (burgundy, chianti, etc.)
1 large green pepper, sliced crosswise
1 large onion, sliced
1 large tomato, sliced
Salt and pepper to taste
Paprika to taste

Place each fish in an aluminum foil package, dot with butter or margarine, and pour wine over it. Cover with green pepper, onion, and tomato slices. Sprinkle with salt, pepper, and paprika and seal. Bury in campfire coals. Test for doneness in 15 minutes. The flesh should flake off the bone when touched with a fork.

You can cook the fish the same way using a Dutch oven or a baking pan covered with aluminum foil. Bake at 325° F. for 25 to 35 minutes.

Two of the best friends we have around a seaside camp are Dan and Inez Morris. We all enjoy the sea, camping, and fishing, and all four of us are writers.

One place the Morrises outshine the Strungs, however, is on the subject of cooking. They've authored a whole raft of cookbooks, and turn out some magnificent meals, both in their Long Beach, L.I., kitchen and on the nearby ocean sands.

247

CAMPING IN COMFORT

The following is one of their favorite—and we think their best—recipes. It's a traditional down-East meal, perfectly suited to the boat camper, or the tent or auto camper who's living near the beach. All the ingredients can be bought commercially, but you'll add a special touch to your clambake if you forage some of the food yourself: a few fish you've caught, clams you've dug, or if you're a skin diver, lobsters you've picked from the floor of the sea.

(A or T) New England-Style Clambake

The traditional New England-style clambake, in which all the food is steamed in a pit over hot rocks and wet seaweed, (if no seaweed, use grass and leaves instead) is an experience that no American should miss. This menu is set up for 6 persons.

> 72 clams, preferably steamers, tied 12 to a bundle in cheesecloth or arranged in throwaway aluminum foil dishes.
> 6 fish steaks or fillets
> 6 lobsters, each weighing about 1¼ pounds
> 6 serving-size pieces of chicken. Keep the pieces small, cut drumstick from thighs and breasts in half.
> 6 ears of corn, husks pulled back, silk removed, washed and husks restored
> 6 medium potatoes, scrubbed and still in their jackets
> Butter

There are a pit to be dug, a fire to be built, and rocks to be preheated. Here's how:

• Scoop out a circular hole in the sand about 3 feet in diameter and about 18 to 24 inches deep.

248

- Line it on all sides with rocks. They must be hard non-porous, heat-holding, and each about the size of a football. Fit them as closely together as possible and make the top as level as can be.
- Sweep the pit clean of all dirt or sand with the broom you brought from home.
- Build a fire. Make sure it is distributed to cover the entire circle of rocks. Keep it burning well, never too high, because its purpose is to heat the rocks, which must be intensely hot in order for the clambake to work. Keep the fire going for at least two hours. Perhaps for longer, but never less.
- When the rocks are hot enough, remove every speck of still-burning wood, ember, coal, and cinder with a broom or rake. You must immediately start cooking.
- Place a 6-inch layer of wet seaweed atop the rocks. Spread it carefully to cover every bit of the pit.
- Working very fast to take advantage of the steam, place your foodstuffs on the seaweed in layers—the clams first, next the lobster, then the fish, chicken, corn, and potatoes.
- Wet some canvas or burlap bags and spread them over the pit, anchoring the cloth down well with a ring of stones, and making sure that no gaps remain for steam to escape. It's a good idea to cover the tops of the rocks lining the pit with a layer of seaweed to keep them from burning the canvas.
- In about an hour, everything should be ready for the table. A good way to tell is by carefully lifting up an edge of the canvas on the side of the pit that's away from the wind and looking at the lobster. If it's red all over, melt plenty of butter and get in line.

(A) Barbecued Ribs

3 pounds beef short ribs or pork spare ribs
3 tablespoons bacon fat

2 cups barbecue sauce
½ cup brown sugar
Salt and pepper to taste

Melt bacon fat in a heavy skillet. Salt and pepper the ribs and brown them in bacon fat. Place in a 9-by-12 roasting pan and sprinkle half of the brown sugar on the ribs. Pour the barbecue sauce over the ribs and top with the rest of the brown sugar. Bake at 375° F. for 1½ hours or until done.

(T) Norm's Barbecued Roast

1 5–7-pound beef roast
1 cup barbecue sauce
¼ cup brown sugar
Salt and pepper to taste

Wipe meat with damp cloth and rub with salt and pepper. Combine barbecue sauce and brown sugar, and baste meat with it. Place on grill or on skewer for spit. Turn frequently and keep basting till meat is done to your liking. Cooking time 1½ to 2 hours depending on heat of coals.

(T) Barbecued Pork Chops in Mushroom Sauce

6 pork chops
½ cup water
1 10½-ounce can undiluted cream of mushroom soup
Pepper to taste

Arrange chops on grill, sprinkle with pepper, and cook 4 to 6 inches above coals for 15 minutes to a side or until nicely browned and almost cooked. Remove from grill, lay chops on sheets of heavy-duty aluminum foil, 2 to a sheet. Add can of water to mushroom soup, stir until smooth, and spread over chops. Wrap and seal chops with the foil and lay packages on grill 4 to 6 inches above coals. Cook for 20 minutes, turning over after 15 minutes. *Serves 4 to 6.*

(T) Meat Kabobs

½ slices of bacon, folded
    Whole mushroom caps
    Onion chunks
    Small potatoes, cooked
    Green pepper chunks
1½-inch chunks of sirloin, veal, lamb, or pork
    Salt and pepper to taste
    Butter or barbecue sauce

Assemble kabobs by alternating bacon, mushrooms, onions, potatoes, peppers, and meat on 12-inch to 24-inch skewers. Grill over coals until done. Baste with either a butter sauce or your favorite barbecue sauce. To serve: rest end of skewer on plate; with knife, push food off skewer.

For extra flavor, marinate the meat before cooking in Soy Marinade and use the marinade for basting as the kabobs are grilled.

(T) Soy Marinade for Meat Kabobs

¾ cup soy sauce
½ cup red wine
1 tablespoon curry powder

     ¼ teaspoon powdered ginger
     1 clove minced garlic

Combine ingredients. Pour over boneless cubes of meat and let stand overnight in refrigerator or cooler.

(A) Bird and Mushroom Stew

If you're a hunter as well as a camper, here's the perfect dish for the birds you bag. If you're not a hunter, you'll discover some mighty fine things will happen to a chicken cooked this way.

     ½ cup lard or shortening
     2 chickens or pheasant or three grouse
     2 cans condensed cream of mushroom soup
        Salt and pepper to taste
        Italian-flavored bread crumbs

Section birds into serving-sized pieces. Roll pieces in bread crumb mixture seasoned with salt and pepper, and brown in lard. Arrange pieces in a Dutch oven and pour on the mushroom soup. Cover oven and simmer for 2½ hours, or until meat can easily be separated from the bone.

(A) Clams on a Baked Shell

Raw clams on the half shell are tasty treats for any beach camper. But if you've got an oven aboard your boat or recvee, don't overlook baking your clams. They're great as a main dish, and make wonderful hors d'oeuvres.

     1 dozen cherrystone clams, diced (reserve any liquid)

¼ cup bread crumbs
1 teaspoon powdered garlic or 2 cloves chopped garlic
1 teaspoon minced onions
⅛ teaspoon salt
2 tablespoons olive oil
1 teaspoon parsley
Parmesan cheese
½ teaspoon oregano

Sauté garlic, onion, parsley, oregano, and bread crumbs in olive oil for 3 minutes, mixing thoroughly. When onion and garlic start to brown remove mixture from frying pan and mix with clams, clam juice, and salt. Spoon into shells, sprinkle lightly with bread crumbs and Parmesan cheese. Place on baking sheet in 375° F. oven for 25 to 30 minutes until crispy on top.

CAMPING COUNSEL AT HOME AND ABROAD

Campers are popular people. They're so welcome that state, federal, and foreign governments maintain agencies to answer campers' questions, and advise them about such things as the clothes to bring, the facilities they can expect to enjoy, and what there will be to see and do.

The following is a list of agencies you can write to learn about the camping conditions and potentials across our nation and in other lands. The United States comes first—in alphabetical order by state. Next come federal agencies, including our national parks; after that, our closest neighbors, Canada and Mexico; then Europe.

Maybe just one bit of advice is due. When you write

CAMPING IN COMFORT

these agencies, be specific. If you want to know how much gas costs in London, or how many campsites there are in Paris, or when Yosemite Park has the most wild flowers, ask. No one can know your interests and intent until you tell them, or answer a question that wasn't asked. And, of course, when you write, do it well in advance of your camp out.

STATE CAMPING INFORMATION

ALABAMA
Department of Conservation
State Capitol
Montgomery, Alabama 36104

ALASKA
Alaska Travel Division
Pouch E
Juneau, Alaska 99801

ARIZONA
Arizona Development Board
1500 West Jefferson Street
Phoenix, Arizona 85026

ARKANSAS
Arkansas Publicity and
Parks Commission
State Capitol Building
Little Rock, Arkansas 72201

CALIFORNIA
California State Office of
Tourism and Visitors'
Services
926 J Building, Room 812
Sacramento, California 95814

COLORADO
Division of Commerce and
Development
602 State Capitol Annex
Denver, Colorado 80203

CONNECTICUT
Connecticut Parks and
Forest Commission
State Office Building
Hartford, Connecticut 06101

DELAWARE
Delaware State Park
Commission
3300 Faulkland Road
Wilmington, Delaware 19899

DISTRICT of COLUMBIA
National Capital Region
National Park Service
1100 Ohio Drive, Southwest
Washington, D.C. 20242

FLORIDA
Florida Park Service
101 West Gaines Street
Tallahassee, Florida 32304

254

GEORGIA
Georgia Department of
State Parks
7 Hunter Street, Southwest
Atlanta, Georgia 30334

HAWAII
Division of State Parks
P.O. Box 621
Honolulu, Hawaii 96809

IDAHO
Department of Commerce
and Development
State House
Boise, Idaho 83707

ILLINOIS
Illinois Division of Parks and
Memorials
100 State Office Building
Springfield, Illinois 62706

INDIANA
Tourist Division
Indiana Department of
Commerce
State House
Indianapolis, Indiana 46204

IOWA
State Conservation
Commission
State Office Building
300 Fourth Street
Des Moines, Iowa 50319

KANSAS
Kansas Parks and Resources
Authority
801 Harrison Street
Topeka, Kansas 66612

KENTUCKY
Kentucky Department of
Public Relations
Capitol Annex
Frankfort, Kentucky 40601

LOUISIANA
Louisiana Parks and
Recreation Commission
P.O. Drawer 1111
Baton Rouge, Louisiana 70821

MAINE
State Park and Recreation
Commission
State House Office Building
Augusta, Maine 04330

MARYLAND
Department of Forests and
Parks
State Office Building
Annapolis, Maryland 21404

MASSACHUSETTS
Division of Parks and Forests
15 Ashburton Place
Boston, Massachusetts 02108

MICHIGAN
Michigan Tourist Council
Stevens T. Mason Building
Lansing, Michigan 84926

MINNESOTA
Division of State Parks
320 Centennial Office
Building
St. Paul, Minnesota 55101

255

CAMPING IN COMFORT

MISSISSIPPI
  Mississippi State Park System
  1102 Woolfolk Building
  Jackson, Mississippi 39201

MISSOURI
  Missouri Tourism Commission
  308 East High Street
  Box 1055
  Jefferson City, Missouri 65101

MONTANA
  Montana Highway
    Commission
  Helena, Montana 59601

NEBRASKA
  Nebraskaland
  State Capitol
  Lincoln, Nebraska 68509

NEVADA
  Nevada State Park System
  Capitol Building
  Carson City, Nevada 89701

NEW HAMPSHIRE
  New Hampshire Division of
    Economic Development
  P.O. Box 856
  Concord, New Hampshire
    03301

NEW JERSEY
  Department of Conservation
    and Economic Development
  P.O. Box 1889
  Trenton, New Jersey 08625

NEW MEXICO
  New Mexico State Tourist
    Division
  302 Galisteo
  Santa Fe, New Mexico 87501

NEW YORK
  Division of State Parks
  State Campus Site
  Albany, New York 11226

NORTH CAROLINA
  Travel Information Division
  Department of Conservation
    and Development
  Raleigh, North Carolina
    27602

NORTH DAKOTA
  North Dakota Outdoor
    Recreation Agency
  State Office Building
  Bismarck, North Dakota
    58501

OHIO
  Ohio Development
    Department
  Travel and Tourist Division
  Box 1001
  Columbus, Ohio 43216

OKLAHOMA
  Oklahoma Division of
    State Parks
  Room 533
  State Capitol Building
  Oklahoma City, Oklahoma
    73109

OREGON
  Oregon State Highway
    Division
  101 State Highway Building
  Salem, Oregon 97301

PENNSYLVANIA
  State Department of Forests
    and Waters
  Harrisburg, Pennsylvania
    17120

RHODE ISLAND
  Rhode Island Development
    Council
  Roger Williams Building
  Hayes Street
  Providence, Rhode Island
    02908

SOUTH CAROLINA
  Department of Parks,
    Recreation, and Tourism
  P.O. Box 1358
  Columbus, South Carolina
    29202

SOUTH DAKOTA
  Department of Highways
  Travel Division
  Pierre, South Dakota 57501

TENNESSEE
  Tennessee Division of
    State Parks
  235 Cordell Hull Building
  Nashville, Tennessee 37219

TEXAS
  Texas State Parks Board
  Drawer E
  Capitol Station
  Austin, Texas 78701

UTAH
  Utah Tourist and
    Publicity Council
  State Capitol
  Salt Lake City, Utah 84114

VERMONT
  Department of Forests and
    Parks
  Montpelier, Vermont 05602

VIRGINIA
  Department of Recreation
    and Parks
  The Mosque
  Laurel and Main Streets
  Richmond, Virginia 23220

WASHINGTON
  Washington State Parks and
    Recreation Commission
  P.O. Box 1128
  Olympia, Washington 98501

WEST VIRGINIA
  West Virginia Division of
    Parks and Recreation
  State Office Building
  Charleston, West Virginia
    25305

WISCONSIN
  Wisconsin Vacation and
    Travel Service
  Box 450
  Madison, Wisconsin 53701

WYOMING
  Wyoming Recreation
    Commission
  P.O. Box 309
  Cheyenne, Wyoming 82001

CAMPING IN COMFORT

FEDERAL CAMPING INFORMATION

NATIONAL FORESTS:
  Forest Service
  U. S. Department of
    Agriculture
  Washington, D.C. 20240

NATIONAL PARKS:
  National Park Service
  U. S. Department of the
    Interior
  Washington, D.C. 20240

FOREIGN CAMPING INFORMATION

CANADA
  Canadian Government
    Travel Bureau
  Ottawa, Ontario, Canada

MEXICO
  Mexican Government
    Tourism Department
  Reforma 45
  Mexico, D.F.

MEXICAN
GOVERNMENT
TOURISM
  Suite 3508
  630 Fifth Avenue
  New York, New York 10019

EUROPE
  Federation française de
    Camping et de Caravaning
  22, avenue Victoria
  Paris ler, France

DUTY REQUIREMENTS
  For duty requirements when
    entering the U.S., write to:
  Internal Revenue Service
  Washington, D.C. 20240

CAMPING CLUBS

Campers are congenial and gregarious souls, and they like to share their fun with everyone. As a result, camping clubs have been formed and are functioning across the nation.

Many of them are industry sponsored. Manufacturers of tenting equipment and recvees support organizations that are made up of owners of their products. Airstream Corporation, for example, pioneered "caravanning," a cross-country

258

trip of trailer owners who often number in the hundreds. Members cue up at some predetermined meeting place and tow their wheeled homes as a group. These caravans amount to a mobile community, with individual members assigned specific tasks. There's always a doctor in the number, and a person who's chosen "postmaster." He collects and distributes mail to members en route. The caravans also boast social committees, service committees, and even a "caboose." It's the caboose's job to follow up the rear and make sure stragglers aren't stranded. He's usually a mechanic by trade.

Organized thus, Airstream caravans have visited every state in the union and every corner of the globe, and have encouraged other groups to do the same.

But recvee owners aren't the only campers who are climbing on the club band wagon. Conservation-oriented organizations such as the Sierra Club sponsor regular pack trips into the back country for campers whose interests lie with wilderness wandering. Clubs of this kind are particularly beneficial in that many of their members are amateur naturalists, and the information on flora, fauna, and geology they're happy to provide adds a welcome new dimension to the outdoor experience.

And, of course, there are small, private clubs that amount to a loose organization of neighbors who like to get together and shoot the breeze around a campfire, or while viewing last year's slides of Yellowstone.

The benefits of joining a camping club are many. There's of course the association with people who have the same interests as you, but beyond that, the club is a great place to exchange ideas, learn new camping techniques, and is a way for you to have a say in legislative matters that concern campers and outdoorsmen.

Although the list of United States camping clubs is long (and somewhat incomplete because of so many small, local organizations), here's a sampling of the larger groups, both industry related and private. If you want to join an established club, do so by all means. If you'd like to form one with your friends, any group on the list can help you with information and an explanation of how it got its start.

Airstream Caravan Club
  822 Niles St.
  Bakersfield, California 93301

Family Camping Federation
  Bradford Woods
  Martinsville, Indiana 46151

Family Motor Coach Association
  Box 44144
  Cincinnati, Ohio 45244

Florida Family Campers
Association
  355 Circle Drive
  Jacksonville, Florida 32208

Indiana Campers Association
  2222 E. 70th Street
  Indianapolis, Indiana 46220

Michigan Family Campers
Association
  Western Michigan University
  Kalamazoo, Michigan 49001

National Campers and Hikers
Association
  7172 Transit Road
  Buffalo, New York 14221

Sierra Club
  1050 Mills Tower
  San Francisco, California
  94104

Winnebago International
Travelers
  Forest City, Iowa

Wisconsin Campers Association
  Box 4241
  Milwaukee, Wisconsin 53210

Norwegian Caravan Club
  Welhavensgot 5
  Oslo, Norway

OTHER BOOKS YOU MAY FIND USEFUL

BYAM, WALLY, *Trailer Travel Here and Abroad* (David McKay Co., New York, 1960).

CARDWELL, PAUL, JR., *America's Camping Book* (Scribner's Sons, New York, 1969).

CHAPMAN, CHARLES F., *Piloting, Seamanship, Small Boat Handling* (Hearst, New York, 1969).

CROSS, CLIFF, *Mexico Guide* (Martin Supply, 1424 W. Kearny Boulevard, Fresno, California 93706).

ELIEL, LAMBERT, *Trailer Owners Manual* (Trail-R-Club of America, California, 1969).

Europa Camping and Caravanning (Wig Wam, Route 44, Rehoboth, Massachusetts 02769).

JOHNSON, JAMES RALPH, *Advanced Camping Techniques* (David McKay Co., New York, 1967); *Anyone Can Camp in Comfort* (David McKay Co., New York, 1964).

KOLLER, LARRY, *Complete Book of Camping and the Outdoors* (Random House, New York, 1957).

LAUBIN, REGINALD and GLADYS, *The Indian Tipi* (University of Oklahoma Press, Norman, 1957).

MERRILL, W. K., *All About Camping* (Stackpole, Harrisburg, Pennsylvania, 1963).

MIRACLE, LEONARD, *Complete Book of Camping* (Harper & Row, New York, 1961).

MORRIS, DAN and INEZ, *The Complete Outdoor Cookbook* (Hawthorn, New York, 1970).

MORRIS, DAN, and NORMAN STRUNG, *Family Fun on and Around the Water* (Cowles, New York, 1970).

261

CAMPING IN COMFORT

NEWMAN, JAMES and BARBARA, *The Family Camping Guide* (World, New York, 1967).

Rand McNally Guidebook to Campgrounds (Rand McNally, New York, 1970).

SMALLMAN, ROBERT E., *The Golden Guide to Camping* (Golden Press, New York, 1965).

WELLS, GEORGE S., *Modern ABC's of Family Camping* (Stackpole, Harrisburg, Pennsylvania, 1967).

WELLS, GEORGE and IRIS, *The Handbook of Auto Camping* (Harper & Row, New York, 1954).

Woodall's Trailering Parks and Campgrounds (Woodall, Illinois, 1969).

ZARCHY, HARRY, *Let's Go Camping* (Knopf, New York, 1951).

Notes

Notes

Notes

Notes

Notes

Notes

Notes

Notes

Notes

Notes